A Path Strewn with Sinners

A Devotional Study of Mark's Gospel
& His Race to the Cross

Wade Johnston, Sinner

BOOKS
NEW REFORMATION
PUBLICATIONS

An Imprint of 1517 the Legacy Project

A Path Strewn With Sinners: A Devotional Study of Mark's Gospel and His Race to the Cross.

Published by:
New Reformation Publications
PO Box 54032
Irvine, CA 92619–4032

Publisher's Cataloging-In-Publication Data
(Prepared by The Donohue Group, Inc.)

Names: Johnston, Wade, 1977–
Title: A path strewn with sinners : a devotional study of Mark's gospel and his race to the cross / Wade Johnston, sinner.
Description: Irvine, CA : NRP Books, an imprint of 1517 the Legacy Project, [2017]
Identifiers: ISBN 978-1-945978-44-9 (hardcover) | ISBN 978-1-945978-45-6 (softcover) | ISBN 978-1-945978-43-2 (ebook)
Subjects: LCSH: Bible. Mark—Commentaries. | Bible. Mark—Criticism, interpretation, etc.
Classification: LCC BS2585.53 .J64 2017 (print) | LCC BS2585.53 (ebook) | DDC 226.3/07—dc23

Printed in the United States of America

NRP Books, an imprint of New Reformation Publications is committed to packaging and promoting the finest content for fueling a new Lutheran Reformation. We promote the defense of the Christian faith, confessional Lutheran theology, vocation and civil courage.

Cover design by Joshua Fortuna

To all the sinners I've been called and blessed to forgive in the stead of Christ, to all who have forgiven me through the mercy of the same, and to all who know my sins all too well and yet love me and allow me to serve them, poorly as that might be, as husband, father, son, professor, colleague, coach, and so on. Ma, Dad, Tricia, Maggie, Nick, Ziggy, Ana, and Mieke, as always, nothing I write or accomplish would be possible without you. I don't make it clear enough, but from God's hand into my life you've come as undeserved and ever-abounding gifts.

Contents

Preface

The Holy Gospel according to St. Mark spent years not only as a challenge but indeed as my foe. In the three-year lectionary, a sequence of readings many Lutherans use throughout the church year, Mark is year B. As a new preacher, fresh out of seminary, year B made my life miserable. Week after week, Jesus healed; Jesus cast out a demon, week after week. How was I supposed to preach that? How was I supposed to keep one sermon from serving as a hollow echo of the previous? Mark's Gospel seemed like dry bones, and I felt tasked with trying to give it life. What a fool I was! The opposite proved true. As I slowed down, as I considered the people I encountered there, the circumstances, the words Jesus spoke (He speaks but few of them in Mark's accounts), Mark's Gospel not only came to life for me—indeed, it had always been alive; it is the *viva vox* of God—but brought me to life with it. It sucked me in. Mark bid me to run the race with the cross with and through him. His prose took me by the hand. Like any race, you don't catch all the details the first time through. You are moving quickly, your eyes fixed ahead. But I am not as fit a man as I'd like to be, and so I have a custom after a run. I like to go home and get my bike and slowly ride the path I trod, using the odometer to measure the distance. Sometimes I am surprised to find out that what seemed like a short run was a lot longer than I thought. Sometimes the opposite is true. When that is the case, I am tempted to be disappointed, but in truth, some of my best runs have been those where I worked hardest to go not all that far. Even more, when I went back and walked or rode the path again, I noticed a lot I hadn't the first time, whether twists, or climbs, or cracks in the pavement. I think that can be the case with Mark's Gospel too. It is the shortest of the four in the Scriptures, but its contents are much greater than the pages it fills.

Wade Johnston
Feast of St. Mark
2017

Introduction

The Gospel of the
Homesick Passion Streaker

Mark is a storyteller. It is his gift. Of all the Gospels, Mark's is
out to tell a tale—not a fairytale, not a myth like those of the
Greeks or Romans, not something based on a true story, but
the story of Christ, the tale of the Savior and of the human race.
As a storyteller, Mark takes certain liberties. If he were one of
my students, he would certainly find red marks on his Gospel,
especially for not keeping tense consistent. The best storytellers
can get away with that, though. The best authors get a free pass,
because it's their ability to break the rules that makes them great
and their stories beautiful. At times, Mark reminds me of my
grandfather telling fishing stories when I was little. "So I says,
and he says, you know." Mark loves to talk like that, delights
in it. It's good stuff. It sucks you in. And to honor his ability
to tell a story, I've occasionally (OK, often) taken liberty with
tense throughout as well, not because I am a good storyteller
or a worthy author, but because I think it is the only way to
do Mark's telling of Jesus' ministry justice, to run with him,
to pound this path strewn with sinners on his terms. Mark
doesn't inundate us with details. He doesn't burden his accounts
with the extraneous. He leaves us to fill in the blanks (I picture
the pigs running into Lake Michigan off the cliff at a nearby

park in Milwaukee, for instance), but he does this, not to make any truth of his Gospel negotiable or the events up for grabs, but to drive them home, to plop us into them.

Mark's Gospel is arranged rhetorically. In other words, he put it together to make certain points—points about Jesus. As he does so, Mark loves to make sandwiches—that is, he likes to sandwich events between teachings, or teachings between events (you get the point)—in order to help drive home what Jesus is after at any certain point. That helps make our approach especially fruitful. The sinners with which Jesus' path is strewn are there for a reason. Mark wants us to learn from them. He wants them to drive home and draw us deeper into the gospel of Christ.

Mark's Gospel has a number of themes, but some stand out as especially central. First, Mark loves to retell how outsiders become insiders, outcasts members of Jesus' company, and sinners saints. In keeping with this, Mark focuses especially upon Jesus time in Galilee. This fact is also explained by Peter's likely influence upon Mark's Gospel. Likely written in Rome and for Romans, influenced by Peter, Mark removes the dividing line between Jew and Gentile; Mark sends Jesus north, into Galilee, often into Gentile regions. Here He spends most of our time with Him in Mark's Gospel, rather than in the geographic and cultural center of Jewish religious life. Mark emphasizes Jesus' authority over sin, death, and the devil, and that Jesus has this authority because He is the Messiah and God Himself. In Mark, we meet the divine Jesus, and yet, interestingly, of all the Gospels, here we meet Him at His most human. His personality comes through more than elsewhere. He is sorrowful, angry, joyful, kind. He stoops down to hold children, touches the lame, eats with sinners, rebukes the unfaithful, and overturns tables in the temple. As with other characters in his accounts, Mark, like an impressionist, does not paint every feature with intricate detail; rather, with a broad brush, he produces a picture that sucks us in, that allows us a glimpse of God at His most human. Our encounters are brief but intense, too quick but almost overpowering. Like the disciples, who Mark presents as slow to learn and often wayward, like a toddler learning to walk, we too stumble along as things slowly become clearer, but in dizzying array. Mark doesn't spoon-feed us. He preaches. His Gospel is a collection of sermons and one big sermon giving us the gospel, giving the Word to us, which God inspired him to write down. And this is likely with good reason. It is almost certain that Mark's Gospel is based on the sermons of Peter. Peter preached . . . and through Mark, he still does. With Peter, Mark went through sermons to the cross and back, and now with Mark, we do the same.

Well, we ought not linger too long here. Mark is waiting, and as usual, he is in a hurry and eager to keep us moving along down this path strewn with sinners.

The Good News Goes Forth

Mark 1:1-20

Matthew and Luke begin their Gospels with the origins of the Savior: with His genealogy, His birth, and at least some of His childhood. Not so with Mark. There is no baby Jesus to contemplate, no Simeon, no slaughter of the innocents, no flight to Egypt, no boy Jesus in the temple—no, none of that. Mark sets us squarely at the beginning of the Christ's ministry. We meet John the Baptist, but not with all the detail and backstory Luke provides. No, we meet John doing what John did and not much more. There he is, leather belt around his camel's hair clothing, baptizing and preaching, pointing to the Messiah to come. And then the Messiah comes, literally, to John, for baptism.

John's baptism was a baptism of repentance. Theologians have debated if John's baptism was Baptism. I'll spare you that. It is enough for our purposes to know that John's baptism was a baptism of repentance. Who repents? The innocent need no repentance. Sinners repent. Sinners repent of sin—*original* and *actual* (original: that with which they were born, and actual: those specific sins by which "in thought, word, and deed" they have confirmed their sinful birthright). And Jesus came for baptism—*this* baptism, the sinner's baptism. Why? He had come to save sinners. This ought to have been no surprise. The blood of numerous generations of innumerable beasts cried out as a reminder of that. And yet, though He came to save sinners, He was no sinner, was He? Why a sinner's baptism? St. Paul would tell us later. Mark felt no need to connect all the dots at the moment—it's a race to the cross, after all. St. Paul put it like this: "For our sake he made him to be sin who knew no sin, so that in him we might become the righteousness of God" (2 Corinthians 5:21).

So there we find the Savior, knee-deep in the sinner's water, fulfilling all righteousness for us, for sinners. And what happens? *Immediately* the Father and Spirit join the scene, and the Father preaches, a short sermon, but a central one, truly *the* sermon this world needed and needs to hear, and yet He speaks it, not to those gathered, to us, but to the Son, an encouragement for this Son of God wet with the water of the unimpressive Jordan, who now undertakes His public ministry: "You are my beloved Son; with you I am well pleased" (1:11).

There is a joke I like to tell in class sometimes. In a small town, the local Baptist church was holding a big revival. With great fanfare, the preacher had gathered a crowd at the river through town. A man, drunk, fresh from the bar—a Lutheran, perhaps, I sometimes joke—stumbled across the bridge over the river. Spotting him, the preacher called out, "Brother, have you found Jesus?" The drunk man, confused, answered, "No." The preacher summoned him into the waters and dunked him under. When the now-wet, still inebriated victim of the preacher's well-meant dunking regained his senses, the preacher asked him again, "Brother, have you found Jesus?" The drunk man answered, "No." Twice more this happened. Finally, frustrated, the drunk asked, "Are you sure He fell in here?"

Now, why do I like to tell this joke? First, I think it's funny. Second, though, I think it serves as a helpful reminder that Jesus in fact *is* in the waters of our Baptism, His Baptism, instituted by Him and given to His bride, the Church. As He descended into the Jordan to undertake His saving ministry, beginning His race to the cross, so now, having completed it, He still now descends into the waters of our baptism, the One who became sin for us to become the righteousness of God, which becomes ours through Baptism, through all preaching of the gospel, even when it comes without water.

What happens after Jesus is baptized? What happens to all the baptized still today? The waters bring with them temptation, because the devil need not work on his own and despises nothing more than what he can never have: Christ Jesus, not merely as an idea or a person, but as a Savior—Christ for me, for you. *Immediately* Jesus went from baptism to temptation, from the Jordan to the wilderness. And He went armed as we are, with the promises of God, with His sure Word. And He emerged not as we have but tempted in every way without sin.

As He would do throughout His ministry, as Mark makes abundantly clear throughout His Gospel, He defeated the devil. He outdueled the old, evil foe. And He did that, too, for us. And then for us, too, He emerged, wearied but unvanquished to travel a path strewn with sinners, to race toward the cross as our Jesus. And He does it with a call, a gracious call, and yet an urgent one all the same: "The time is fulfilled, and the kingdom of God is at hand; repent and believe in the gospel" (1:15). God grant it! And so began the gathering of sinners, twelve especially, and that gathering continues still today, in the very same way, through the preaching of that same gospel.

Thus we begin our race to the cross with the Savior down a path strewn with sinners, *fellow* sinners. Along the way, we do well to stop for water breaks, to ponder and get "baptismal," drowning our sins with those whose sins the Lord pardons, rising again to new life with those He restores. We won't have time to take in every vista, to ponder every hook and hill, but at the very least, I pray we get to know some of those who greeted our Lord on His road to the cross and those the Lord greeted with the benefits of it.

From Church with the Demons to Nowhere with Everyone

Mark 1:21-28

After fishing for apostles along the Sea of Galilee, Jesus went with His new posse of religious nonprofessionals to Capernaum, His headquarters of sorts. Upon His arrival, He was responsible for a burst of healings. His divinity was on full display as He used His power as God for the good of those in need. That was not all, though. And that's not how He began His work there. He began by teaching. He entered the synagogue and taught with authority, for He was the Authority. He taught the things of God as God. He preached the Word of God as the Word of God. And the devil couldn't stand it. *Immediately* a man with an unclean spirit, literally *in* an unclean spirit, began to cry out. This man was under the control of this evil spirit and indeed of all evil spirits. We are not told he was a wicked man. We are told he was unclean. Uncleanliness could be the product of one's behavior, but it could also be something to which one fell victim, the result of something out of one's control. Such is the case with sinners. We easily become the devil's prey. Such is the circumstance of sinners in a fallen world. We can often slip into fallen states or situations out of our control.

Regardless, this man in an unclean spirit cried out, and he did so with an unexpected and yet very clear confession. He confessed the truth. The demons that possessed him called a Christ a Christ. They cried out, "Have you come to destroy us? I know who you are—the Holy One of God" (1:24). And the devil does know who Jesus is. The devil even confesses it, on occasion, begrudgingly. But Jesus will never be for the devil what He is for us. Jesus is the devil's God, as He is the God of all, but He is not the devil's Jesus; He is not He who saves for Satan. He is that only for sinners like us. Jesus had little time for the devil's confession, therefore. Jesus rebuked the demon. He shut its mouth, even as He will shut Satan's mouth when he tries to accuse us on the Last Day. He told the demons to come out, and they did what He said, because He's God, and His Word does what it says. This was a sight to see! These were words to hear! This was a "new teaching with authority!" (1:28). That is what Jesus came to do too: to teach, to preach. So while we see healing after healing, exorcism after exorcism, we do well to remember that He is teaching, even as He does such things, and that it is for the sake of His teaching, and as an outflow of it, that He does the same. While Mark's Gospel lacks the sheer volume of red letters we find in Matthew's or Luke's, Jesus' teaching is central to the book. First, how Jesus teaches is crucial. He teaches with authority. Second, what Jesus teaches is central. He teaches good news, especially to those broken, outcast, undone, overwhelmed—in other words, to those desperately ready to listen.

Immediately Jesus left the synagogue. He went to the home of His friends and apostles Simon (Peter) and Andrew. Perhaps He wanted to rest. Surely, He had reason to think He would escape the throng His growing fame had produced for Him. But here, in the house of friends, Jesus encountered another sinner in need, Simon's mother-in-law. She was sick with a fever. The prognosis does not seem to have been all too positive. Jesus wasn't blind. He also, however, was no show-man. We are simply told that He took her by the hand and lifted her up. And that's all it took. Here we notice a peculiar thing about our Jesus. He is not afraid to take hold of the sick or unclean. He doesn't fear their contagion. He does not recoil in the face of infirmity. Jesus reaches out. He touches. As we will see with lepers, Jesus even does this with the most untouchable.

And so He took hold of Peter's poor mother-in-law, ill with a great fever—ancient-speak for a very serious one. And that did it. She was healed. She was healed, and she got up and did what? She served. She served freely. She had been freed from her fever, and now she freely served the One who had freed her and His disciples. The same is true still today. We are set free, not to sin, but from sin. We are lifted up to serve, not by compulsion, but as free servants of all.

Jesus didn't get His rest. The city was astir. He had set it astir. And so they brought to Jesus "all who were sick or oppressed by demons" (1:32). Imagine the scene. This was a crowd, and a motley crowd at that. The limp, the hopeless, and the possessed pressed in pleading for rescue. "The whole city was gathered together at the door" (1:33). And Jesus healed many. He cast out many demons. He showed mercy as is His very nature. But the demons were not to speak. They were not those whose mouths He had come to open in praise. That was saved for sinners, for sinners were the ones He had come to save.

Having withdrawn to pray, having moved on, now meandering through Galilee, Jesus was met by a leper. It's hard for us to imagine life as a leper. We are more con-nected than ever before. Sickness and death are as hidden as in any age in the past. The sight of a leper would likely bring us to sickness, a few days in their disconnected life to despair. God in His wisdom had taught the Jews the practice of quarantine long before modern medicine. In many ways, the Old Testament laws regarding uncleanliness served as a hedge against pandemic. While that prevented disease from spreading as quickly and as far as it otherwise might have, quarantine did little for those who fell prey to disease. Lepers lived alone—well, virtually alone. They often lived in colonies with other lepers. Misery loves company, and there was much to go around. They were separated from loved ones. They were removed from the community. They were outcasts, their bodies slowly rotting, stinking more, functioning less. Should someone come too close, they had to make their presence known. They had to announce what they were: unclean. Imagine that. That was their social *interaction*. That was their identity. That was their confession: unclean. And the leper we encounter with Jesus had had enough. He came *to* Jesus.

Perhaps you can imagine just a little bit how the leper felt at that moment. Perhaps you've found yourself cut off for a time. Perhaps you've lost your moorings, cut ties, or had ties cut for you without any say. Perhaps you have convinced yourself you are too unclean and that there is no way you dare approach Jesus, let alone a church building, a pastor, or a Christian friend. Perhaps you've spent your days with nothing but your mind mulling what is wrong with you, how unworthy you are, how removed you've become from who you were, and how disenchanted you are with who you are now. Perhaps you can identify.

The leper came to Jesus. He summoned the courage. He risked the embarrassment and heartbreak of the Son of David's rejection. He dared, he was boldly humble, and Jesus didn't rebuke him; the last thing Jesus could have brought Himself to do was to reject him. The man knelt and begged, "If you will, you can make me clean" (1:40). What a prayer! We do well to follow suit with this beggar. Brought to his knees by sickness and isolation, reeking of death, he abandoned himself before the Savior, and the Savior didn't recoil, didn't rebuke, didn't even, so far as we are told, shift His gaze or cover His nose. No, Jesus' guts churned. He got sick to His stomach. His inmost being ached, but not with repulsion; no, He was filled with pity. Compassion consumed Him. So moved was He that when He spoke, it was short and sweet. Tersely yet effectually, He said, "I will; be clean" (1:41). And the leper was. He was clean. He was cleaner than he'd ever been and ever could have been. But Jesus charged him not to tell anyone. Jesus had come to die and rise, not to be a country faith healer, not to be an earthly king. The man, however, couldn't contain his excitement. He went out and spread the word. So Jesus withdrew to the middle of nowhere. Yet even there, people found Him. Nowhere always became somewhere when Jesus arrived on the scene.

A Paralytic, a Tax Collector, and a Physician

Mark 2:1–12

We next stumble upon Jesus "at home" in Capernaum (2:1). Once again it would be quite reasonable that He might have been hoping for some downtime, a while away from the crowds and the demands of life as a new spiritual celebrity. Fame was something the Savior never sought, after all. Quiet time just wasn't in the cards, however. Indeed, things got interesting very quickly. Many had gathered together. It was a tumultuous scene, bodies pressed against each other. Think maybe of a time you've left a stadium after a big event. Body presses against body. There is a wave of humanity. And into this scene came a paralytic. No, he didn't walk there; he was a paralytic. Rather, while he didn't have control of his body, he did have one of life's greatest gifts: he had friends, people who cared enough about him to bring him to Jesus. He had friends who had faith. Jesus makes that clear. What sort of faith did he have? We are left to guess at that. Mark doesn't say for sure. But his friends believed. They knew Jesus could do something. And sometimes that is our strength too. That is *the mutual consolation of brethren*, as the Lutheran Confessions sometimes call it.

What had Jesus been doing up to this point? He had been preaching. Mark's Jesus is a preacher, as much as his Gospel seems to focus on Jesus' deeds. What was Jesus preaching? Mark apparently didn't think we'd have to think too hard to guess. Jesus preached the gospel. He preached the Word, and into the midst of this preaching the paralytic was brought, and he became part of the sermon.

In college, I had a surgery for which I was given a spinal tap and some wonderful medicine to make me forget what was happening. Afterward, I woke up and had one of the strangest experiences of my life. I felt my hand on something strange. I wondered what it was and, only after a few moments, realized it was my leg. My legs were numb. Having the maturity and sense of humor of a college male, I smacked my legs hard a few times, laughing because it didn't hurt. If my friends had been there, I am sure I would have let them punch my legs too. After a while, though, I felt panicked. I was supposed to be able to feel my legs. When would I feel my legs again? Was something wrong? How would I walk?

The man carried by his friends to Jesus' house today was numb. You could have stuck a knife in his feet, and he wouldn't have known the difference. He was in a hopeless situation, and even today, a cure would be unlikely. There was nothing funny about his situation. He was numb for good, so far as he knew. Put yourself on his mat, catching bouncing glimpses of everything as he was carried along, seeing flashes of all kinds of different faces, many of them desperate faces, perhaps many of them faces of children much too young to know sickness like that which had befallen them. His ears would have caught the shouts of joy of the healed and shouts of pain of those still suffering. The crowd must have smelled like a frat house mixed with a gym and a bathroom. The sun beat down on his face as they climbed the roof. All the while, he cooked in the sun like a burger in the heat tray at McDonald's. Then he was lowered into the room, which was a jumble of comfort and confusion, insanity and asylum. And then, before he could even really study the face of this Jesus everyone surged toward like a soccer crowd, Jesus spoke.

Before we consider Jesus' words, though, what do you think the paralytic thought was his biggest problem that day? What do you think the crowd thought was his biggest problem as he was brought forth, lowered through the roof—an interesting detail! As he descended from above, surely those who saw him and knew him assumed that he was there to be healed, that his paralysis was his biggest need. It's understandable, right? We often think that way too. Our health, work, family, and so on struggle or fail, and what becomes our primary concern? What becomes our utmost need? We each must often answer for ourselves, but I'll be the first to confess that at such times my chief and predominant prayer is not for forgiveness, at least not all the time, nor nearly often enough.

Returning to the roof for a moment, it's easy to get caught up in the outrageousness of the manner in which the paralytic was brought to Jesus, isn't it? I mean, they took apart someone's roof, Peter's roof! Can you imagine the apostle watching? What was Jesus' response? It's so attention-grabbing. It's fantastic. It's the stuff of a great story. And yet—and yet—that was not what proved to be most amazing or stood out the most. What got everyone's attention and showed who was and wasn't a real disciple and an authentic believer in the promises of the Old Testament? It was what Jesus said. It was the absolution He spoke, not as a called servant of Christ, not in God's stead, but as Christ, as God. And we dare not lose the sheer overwhelming shock of that, because the same Jesus who forgave the sins of the paralytic forgives ours too, even when we have trouble keeping that need foremost in our considerations, even when those sins seem too sinful, too repeated, too public, or too irreligious. Those words still define who Jesus is for the Church and all people, still separate disciples from religious posers, still reveal faith or expose a lack of it; those words still pack power and present Jesus as He came to be, is, and shall remain: our Jesus who came to save sinners, who came to show mercy. His words were offensive to those who would not have Him, and He made them as offensive as they could be. The verb Jesus uses here for forgiving could not be clearer or more offensive to his opponents. Jesus is saying that right there, right then, by Him, the man's sins are forgiven. This is not some statement about what God does or is doing in their presence as some sort of an abstraction. The statement makes clear that God, *Jesus*, is right there, in person, doing this, what only God can do.

Jesus' opponents didn't ask a bad question. They were right; only God can forgive sin. It was the answer they got wrong or didn't like. They could not believe Jesus was God, or they wouldn't believe it, because He wasn't the god they wanted. He did not fit their *idea* of God. An *idea* of God is a nice thing. It's comfortable. It has no rough edges. It can be molded, polished, shaved, and embellished. We like *ideas*. We control them. But God is not an idea. Jesus is a person, and there He was, and there He is, still today, in Word and Sacrament, forgiving sin, like it or leave it. Both the paralytic and Jesus' opponents walked out of Peter's house that day, but only one of them walked away forgiven, because he had come with no illusions, with nothing to offer but need, with no hope but gospel. He'd been physically numb, but Jesus' accusers remained something much worse: spiritually numb. They were numb to their need for a Savior. They were numb to the love of God made man, who would be crucified for sinners. There is no worse, no more deadly numbness than that.

Calling a Tax Collector and Supping with Sinners

Mark 2:13-17

What comes next seems unfathomable—if we try to fathom it, that is. It can be too easy to just read on and pass by in this race to the cross. But Mark included it here for a reason. It's a nod to another evangelist. It's also an account—a very brief account—of the power of gospel invitation. Jesus went out again along the sea, and as usual, a crowd surrounded Him. As He was wont to do, He began to preach. What did He preach? Mark expects you to be able to figure that out. And then as Jesus moved along His way, He stumbled upon a sinner. Tax collectors were one of the chief sinners in Jesus' time. They were extortionists, banking on how much they thought they could shake out of their neighbors, and traitors, taking money from the Jews and giving it to their Roman occupiers. Tax collectors aren't popular today. Imagine what it must have been like under the circumstances back then. Perhaps some expected Jesus to rebuke the man. This is the first time we stumble upon a tax collector at a toll booth on this path after all. It would have made sense for the Messiah, the hero of Israel, to put such a man in his place. And yet what do we hear the Savior speak? Jesus says, "Follow me" (2:14). Notice that there is no question mark.

Notice that there are no details. There is just "Follow me."
"Where?" it might be natural to ask. Or "Why?" or "Now?"
or "For how long?" But what do we read? What does Mark
see fit to tell us? It's four words in the Greek: "And he popped
up and followed him" (2:14).

That is fantastical, isn't it? It is hard to believe that a man
would just leave everything without questions and follow some
guy from a town he's perhaps never visited or heard of, a man
traveling with a religious B-team, opposed by the experts of the
day. What did this Jesus have that he hadn't found elsewhere,
not even in the synagogue? You know the answer. It's what Jesus
had when He called you in the same way. When as an infant,
unable to speak, walk, and perhaps even process who you
were and what was happening, He came to you in the waters
of Baptism and said, "Follow me," and here you are. When you
had finally had enough of everyone else's promises, of bot-
tles or banknotes or the banality of platitudes and packaging,
and someone preached to you, the Word took you by the ear,
and said "Follow me." When you had been broken, hit rock
bottom, been left empty, and someone picked you up, showed
you the love of Christ, and that love bid you, "Follow me."
Whatever it was, whatever brought you here, or wherever this
might bring you, the same words have been, are being spoken to
you: "Follow me." And the gospel does what it commands. This
isn't the law. This isn't negotiation. There is no please or thank
you. There is God, God who loves you, speaking words you can't
but trust through the Spirit's gracious intercession. You couldn't
do it otherwise, but when He takes hold of you, when He takes
the reins, there is nothing else to do. No, you've not been called
to be an apostle. You've been called to be you, where you are, in
the roles and jobs (vocations) in which God has plopped you.
You have not been called to leave all—although sometimes we
are called to do that. Whatever the case, though, you have been
called, and you have followed, or you will follow—that's right, if
you are reading unsure you stand with Jesus, beware. His Word
is no vain echo or hapless babbling; it is powerful and effective,
prying even tax collectors from their profits.

Jesus didn't stop there. He upped the ante and went to eat at Levi's (Matthew's) house! He went there to eat with Levi's friends—*sinners*! It was quite the scene. Levi's wretched network of outcasts and Jesus' disciples. (Mark adds here, "And you know, there were a lot.") There Jesus sat, flouting all that many considered most holy, associating with a basket of deplorables. The scribes of the Pharisees were predictably incensed, and yet they didn't go to Jesus. They worked through His disciples. Perhaps they were more reasonable than this odd purveyor of grace and mercy, this friend of sinners. "He's eating with sinners and tax collectors!" they pointed out. The disciples should have known that well already. They were sinners after all. The Gospels leave little doubt about that. Even more, consider what such a statement implies. What weren't these Pharisees? They weren't sinners, or so they thought. How sad! How tragic, like a man who refuses to admit his cancer, even as it ravages his flesh, and therefore refuses treatment.

Jesus heard this nonsense—indeed, "The strong don't need a doctor, but the sick" (2:17). And that is what the Pharisees thought they were: strong. They could handle their salvation. In fact, they didn't need salvation, they thought, but were due for wages, for rewards. They were nailing the whole "righteousness" thing. God was lucky to know them, to count them as His own. But God didn't count them as His own. God was sitting right there, eating with sinners, and they wanted nothing to do with Him. They didn't have ears to hear. Like a bodybuilder in the gym, they were busy staring at their own spiritual muscles. They saw no reason to seek help. Despair was a foreign concept. They were set, well, and good.

> Jesus continued, "I have come to call sinners, not the righteous" (17). Are you a sinner? Luther once counseled a troubled friend, before the 95 Theses even:
>
>> Now I should like to know if your soul, tired of its own righteousness, is learning to be revived by and to trust in the righteousness of Christ. . . . Beware of aspiring to

such purity that you will not wish to be looked upon as a sinner, or to be one. For Christ dwells only in sinners. On this account he descended from heaven, where he dwelt among the righteous, to dwell among sinners. Meditate on this love of his and you will see his sweet consolation.[1]

You'd better be a sinner. You'd better have no illusions about it. Indeed, irreligious and even blasphemous as it sounds, you'd better rejoice in the fact. Go ahead, shout it: "I am a sinner!" No, don't delight in your sin. Your sin will damn you. No, don't delight in your sinfulness. You cannot escape it on your own, and it is killing you. No, rather, delight to be the very one Christ has come to call, to save, and to pull from the gutter and dress with His gown. "I am a sinner, and Christ has come *for me*. I am a sinner, and don't you dare tell me I am not a saint, for I am Christ's and He is mine!" That was the joy that moved Levi to follow. That was the glee that led him to gather his circle of fellow sinners to meet his Jesus. That is what gives life to our dry bones and makes our hands and feet, our mouths and hearts extensions of the Savior's own. Those who came to Jesus as righteous were not righteous at all. They were frauds, phonies, fools. But those who came as sinners, theirs was the righteousness of God. They were salt and light and everything the world needs and everything the self-righteous could never be, no matter how much they claimed or how hard they tried. The same is true today. Stop striving for gifts. Gifts are given. Rejoice that Christ gives you Himself and all that is His. Live by it, or you have no life at all. The Physician has come. Take His medicine with joy.

---

[1] LW 48, 12–13. This is cited in Scott H. Hendrix, *Martin Luther: Visionary Reformer* (New Haven: Yale University Press, 2015), 47.

A Withered Hand, Confessing Demons, and Sleeper Picks

Mark 3:1–6, 13–19

Jesus wasn't done having fun with the religious elite. We encounter Him next again in the synagogue. There He found a man with a withered hand. What is the normal response when you see a man with such a condition? Perhaps revulsion, but hopefully sympathy, yes? Regardless of your disposition, you might find yourself staring, but Jesus' opponents had their eyes fixed on him for another reason. They wanted to see if Jesus would heal on the Sabbath. It shouldn't have been a question at all. He was Jesus, the friend of sinners, driven by mercy, moved by compassion. And it wasn't a question for Jesus. It was a given. It was healing given to a man in need. It was also a teaching moment. This healing preached. The Sabbath wasn't a line item on a check list, a time established for pompous and deluded presumed piety. The Sabbath had a purpose, and Jesus had come to give it, to be our Sabbath, our rest. When Jesus saw that His opponents would begrudge this man healing, he was angry. Even more, He was grieved. He was grieved by their hardness of heart. Once again, He didn't need many words to make His point. The Sabbath was for hearing the Word, and Jesus, the Word, needed few words to remind them who He was and why He came. "Stretch out your hand," He said—an unreasonable request to a man with a withered hand. But just as Jesus' "Follow me" gave what it bid, so also this. The man extended his withered hand, and it was restored, and *immediately* His opponents set to destroying Jesus. It is amazing how we can despise those who would help us, how we can hold rescue in contempt. Jesus was a problem for them, however. And people have taken issue with His mercy ever since. Humanity would rather be left alone, abandoned to its misdirected desires. It can have its way, but not without stumbling over Jesus, who came down to heaven to throw a wrench in our selfish and destructive thinking, who put our best interest first in order to free us from our self-interest.

We'll leave much of the remainder of the chapter for your personal study, but it is worth noting here again that the demons confess Jesus. No, they don't confess Jesus *for them*, but they do confess who He is, His person, His office. And yet it did and does them no good. It is one thing to know there is a Jesus, to believe He is the Christ. It is quite another to know He is Jesus *for me*, that He is *my* Christ. And yet that is what He is. He is Jesus *for you*. He is *your* Christ, unimportant and unworthy as you feel at times. The demons are no friends, but even they were moved to confess who Jesus was. How much more ought we confess who He is *for us*, not in some subjective, personal, relative sort of way, but absolutely, objectively, indisputably, bound by His promise, stubborn in His Word.

Mark also includes here the calling of the Twelve. We need not belabor it, but it is worth noting that while Jesus called men who would be faithful, who would give their lives for Him in the end, He did not call those whom most would have expected. He called very human humans. He called men with obvious flaws. He chose apostles who would for a time scatter, who would often be slow to listen and learn, frequently too enamored of glory to contemplate His cross, at least in this part of the race. And yet He called them. And in Him we commemorate them. We give thanks for them. They were something special because of Jesus. And the same is true for us. Whatever our vocations, we are something special; our daily tasks and personal struggles are imbued with purpose and hallowed in Jesus. Our names too are remembered, for they are written in the book of life and will be called by God Himself when the time is ripe. All this is so, not because we chose Him, not because of who we were, but because He has chosen us, because of who we are as His baptized children.

Riders in the Storm

Mark 4:35–41

Jesus had spent a lot of time teaching before we arrive with Him on the sea. And His teaching had centered in persistence in the faith, by the Word, preached and administered. Through parables, He had extolled the power of God-given faith in the gospel and the precariousness of those whose grasp on the good news was tenuous, ill-fed, or self-serving. Now, after all this teaching, He set out to sea with fishermen, men seasoned on rough waters. He set out for some time alone, for rest, for quiet.

Boats and God don't go together well, though. Water isn't the problem. Jesus walked on water. Moses walked through the Red Sea. Joshua walked across the Jordan. The issue seems to be more with boats. When God judged the earth in the flood, Noah was holed up in a giant ship that he built while being mocked by the neighbors whose carcasses later floated by him. Jonah boarded a boat to escape God's call to go to Nineveh but ended up in the belly of a giant fish. St. Peter left a boat to walk on water, which went well for a while before he thought through what he was doing and sank. St. Paul was shipwrecked on a boat to Rome and bitten by a snake. When God tells you to get in a boat, or out of a boat, testing and trouble seem to be the order of the day.

Yet when Jesus told the disciples to get in a boat with him and cross over to the other side of the Sea of Galilee, a sea known for the nasty tempests that could kick up without notice from time to time, they got in and went. They took Jesus out to sea, just as He was, no questions asked. Faith was pretty easy when all seemed well. But they would soon learn what Noah, Jonah, and later, St. Paul learned all too well: boat plus God equals a test of faith.

When I was younger, my parents sprung for fancy swimming lessons for me. My uncle and my father, whom I love, threw me in my aunt's pool and told me I could swim. I couldn't swim. At least, I didn't think I could swim. But, you know what, when sink or swim came, I learned I could swim. Sure, Dad and Uncle Jeff would have saved me if I'd sunk . . . I think, but that didn't mean that I shouldn't be tossed in the water. So also, Jesus saved St. Peter when he sank, but that didn't mean that he didn't learn by taking those first few steps of faith off of the boat.

Years later, I realized that this is the same way the very little are sometimes taught to swim—infants who, individually, are probably not as big of a baby as I was. My cousin learned to swim that way. It was amazing. They tossed these little kids in, and they just took off like fish. Of course, they had been taught to hold their breath, to go under water, to paddle and so forth earlier, but they still had to get wet in a big way to learn the lesson. So also, Jesus had just been preaching and teaching, explaining parables to the disciples, before they got into the boat. But sometimes Christians have to get wet in a big way for the lesson to really take hold.

The Christian life is one of faith. The Bible tells us this repeatedly and clearly. The Christian Faith is taught with the Word, that is most certainly true. The Faith is based on historical facts and figures. The Faith is learned, but unfortunately, it is not tested like algebra or chemistry. It is tested in the water. It is tested with times when our will, our ability,

our capacity to do anything to save ourselves or fix the problem has been tossed out the window and we must rest alone
in God's will, His ability, and His capacity to save, revealed in
Christ. Faith is trust, not a rational decision. All our planning
and plotting gets blown away when a tempest too great for us
to weather alone comes along.

At first glance, it would seem the disciples passed the
test. After all, what should faith do in times of turmoil besides
look to Christ? And that is what they did. They turned to
Christ to save them. They held out hope that there was something He could do to help, even if it was straining at the oar
with them. We would expect Jesus to wake up and praise
them. But no, just the opposite happens.

Jesus was tired. You know the feeling. He had been
preaching, teaching, traveling, healing, and so forth. He had
been in the sun all day. He was tired. Who can blame Him?
And like a lot of tired people, Jesus didn't want to be woken,
especially unnecessarily.

And that is where we can get distracted or confused.
How did the disciples wake Him unnecessarily? He was
sleeping. They wanted Him to save them. Obviously, they
had to wake Him up, right?

Nope.

They needed to go back to Jesus' claims about Himself
just as we readers need to go back to what John the Baptist
said about Him at the beginning of Mark's Gospel, remem-
bering who it was sleeping in their boat, seasick, perhaps,
resting in the place in the boat that would move the least, so
human was He, even as He was about to make His divinity
clear in a brief and yet powerful display.

How easy it is to lose Jesus' divinity in His humanity, in
His simplicity and run-of-the-mill-ness at times! He sleeps,
so we assume we must wake Him to save us. He is so like
us, and so we forget how different He is in His similitude.
Think back to Christmas. Remember some of the verses

we sing so joyfully then: "This is he whom heav'n taught singers Sang of old with one accord; Whom the Scriptures of the prophets Promised in their faithful word. Now he shines, the long-expected; Let creation praise its Lord" (*Christian Worship* 35). He who sleeps is He who reigns from all eternity. He who takes His pillow and rests in the stern is He who sees all, knows all, possesses all power, and uses all power to save. He is true God, begotten of the Father from eternity, and true man, born of the Virgin Mary. He is weak to take our place. He is strong to save.

Jesus had come to save. He had to die on a cross, not drown on the bottom of the sea. With Him, the disciples were safe. They didn't need to wake Him. It was enough that He was in the boat. He was their guarantee of life. Whether he slept or strained at the oar, He was the One through whom the seas were made and by whom the ocean's boundaries were set. Asleep or awake, the eyes, ears, and heart beating with love of His divinity were active and in no need of rest. Weak faith awoke the Savior, and weak faith received its salvation. Strong faith would have let Him sleep and ridden the storm out. Strong faith too would have received salvation. The Savior doesn't begrudge them their weak faith—He answers its plea and muzzles, as the Greek indicates, the raging storm, as a master might muzzle a barking dog keeping the neighbors awake—but exhorts them to stronger faith. Both weak faith and strong faith look to Jesus. Both save. Let that be clear. Even the tiniest sliver of faith in Jesus is powerful, for it is faith *in Jesus*. And yet our faith in specific promises can be stronger. We do have moments where our trust seems firmer. Christ is never more or less firm, but our trust appears that way. Still, the answer isn't to suck it up, to pull ourselves up by our bootstraps, to try really, really hard to believe, as if we were some Jedi trying to move something with our mind. The answer is to look to Jesus, to remember He is

Jesus, whether sleeping or awake, and to cling to His promises and expressed purposes.

There is a debate about the origins of Aran Knitting,
a particular style of knitting from Ireland. Some propose a
noble and colorful history. Others are more benign. As
you might guess, the story of the noble and colorful ori-
gin is more interesting. Here it is. Irish families out of love
knit sweaters with a waterproof knitting style and a unique
design to mark them with their family's design, which, by
the way, made it easier to identify bodies when they washed
ashore. Christ also has us dressed in a waterproof robe of
His righteousness, proven in Baptism when we lived in the
same waters in which our old Adam was drowned. And
the family seal has been placed upon you, not that God
might bury you when you wash ashore, but so that He might
claim your body to raise it by the same power that brought
our crucified Savior from the grave. No storm can swallow
those dressed in Christ.

Luther said a proverb for the Church should be that
Christ is in the boat, even if He's sleeping, and that is really
all that matters. Remember that the difference between the
unbeliever and the Christian is not that one has troubles
and the other doesn't—we all will have our storms—but
that the Christian knows that Christ is in the boat, even
if He sleeps. That storm was good for the disciples. Three
of four Gospels record it for that reason. Mark didn't have
to include it, but he did. Storms can be good for you as
well. They can fix your eyes on Christ. You ever look up
in church? Many churches look like an upside boat. You
sit in the nave—a word related to our word "navy." The
Church is God's ark, weathering tempest and trial with
Jesus at the head, even when He sleeps and we strain at
the oar. At times, we might wish He would do something
more spectacular than rest in bread and wine and speak
promise through a guy in a robe, but it has always been

enough and always will be enough for the Church to know that, no matter how loud the winds howl or the waves crash, Christ is in the boat, even though He sleeps. And He is in the boat, so you can sleep in peace as well, even while storms rage.

The Only Sane Man in Gerasenes

Mark 5:1-20

This is one of my favorite accounts in all of Scripture, and this chapter is one of the most powerful in all of Mark's Gospel. It's simply packed with his key themes and emphasis. Christ has come for sinners—all sinners. He has authority over sin, death . . . and the Gentile. He races from one healing to another. He mends the most broken. It is wonderful! Here we see Jesus going full Jesus in a way perhaps only surpassed by His passion.

We next travel with Jesus to Gentile country. The pigs are evidence of that. We sometimes forget one of the wonderful blessings of being New Testament believers: bacon! We race with Jesus to Gentile country, and there we find a most odd welcome. *Immediately* Jesus was confronted by a demoniac, a man in an unclean spirit. This was the welcoming committee—a crazy man. Everything about this man is disheveled. He lives in the tombs, and surely smells like them. No one could bind him. But why would they want to? Well, they had tried, again and again, because he was out of his mind, he was in an unclean spirit, and he was, as many would diagnose it today, insane. They couldn't bind him, even with chains. They had bound him with shackles by his legs, and it did nothing. No one could control him. He broke any fetters. He threw off anyone who took hold of him. He wasn't only crazy; he was crazy strong. Moreover, he was naked, at least it would seem. Later those who see him are surprised he is clothed. There must have been a reason for that. It was out of the ordinary, in other words. This crazy, smelly, violent, uncontrollable man welcomes Jesus, runs up to confront Him. What might be a reasonable response? Fear, anger, and a threat of retaliation should he place a hand on Jesus or His disciples?

At this point, something very interesting happened. Sometimes Mark puts confessions in the mouths of demons, but here he places these words not in the mouths of the demons that possessed him, and there were a lot of them, but in the man himself, or at least the antecedent indicates that. The man in an unclean spirit says—no, yells, "Why are you sticking your nose in my business, Jesus, Son of the Most High God? Don't torture me, I tell you!" (5:9). And he kept begging too.

And here, the story—the true story, of course—gets even more fascinating. In 2005, I did a very pastoral thing: I clipped an article from a newspaper. What newspaper? I don't know anymore, but I know it was 2005, because I wrote that. Why did I clip the story? Like many pastors, I liked to store away things that might serve as good sermon illustrations. The story goes like this. The headline reads, "450 sheep jump to their deaths in Turkey." Tell me that wouldn't grab your attention! Even greater (should I not laugh every time I read this?), it begins, "First one sheep jumped to its death." That is the lead sentence—the whole sentence. Talk about a commentary on sheep as a species, and to think God compares us to these creatures again and again and again! My favorite line reads, "In the end, 450 dead animals lay on top of one another in a billowy white pile." Next they interviewed one of the shepherds. Can you imagine? What must have it been like to watch this happen, to look at that "billowy, white pile"? How would you even begin to describe it? We find something similar along our path today.

Nearby was a herd of pigs—because it was a Gentile region, and for the Jews before Christ, remember, no bacon. This wasn't just a tiny herd of pigs. There were about two thousand. That's a lot of pigs if you were wondering. Now, if you've been around pigs, you know they are neither quiet nor unassuming creatures. During my vicar year (an internship year in some Lutheran church bodies), my wife and I, along with our oldest daughter, then a toddler, lived on a pig farm. It took some getting used to, let me tell you. First, of course, there was the smell, but even more unsettling was the noise. During the night, the pigs would scream, as if someone was getting murdered. I'm from Detroit, so I was used to it, but it took a while for my wife to learn to sleep through it. (I joke; I am from Detroit, and I love it, and it is on a big rebound, and you should totally visit!) Imagine the commotion of this herd, then. Imagine the way it must have struck the senses. And then what happened? The herd took off, mad with demons, and the devil worked all that he can really work in the end—that is, destruction and death. The pigs plunged headfirst into the sea and were drowned—about *two thousand* of them. And here my imagination gets the better of me. Did they float? Did local boys jump from pig to pig? How big was the heap of them? What went through the herdsmen's minds? How would they explain it to the boss? Just think about it. Mark fills in none of the blanks, though.

Next thing we know, we're standing with the townspeople, drawn to the scene by the report of the herdsmen. And, oh yeah, that crazy demoniac is there too, but he's not crazy; he's "in his right mind, and he's not a demoniac, and he's wearing . . . clothes" (5:15). What would you expect to come next? They marveled and hailed Jesus as the Messiah. They brought out all their sick and afflicted? They fell to the ground in fear? Nope. None of that. Rather, they begged Jesus to get out of there, to leave the whole region. And Jesus listened. Sometimes God gives us what we want—may He spare us! There are few things more dangerous than to be left to our fallen will. Jesus listened and headed for the boat, and the only sane man in Gerasenes, the naked guy they couldn't chain up who spent his nights cutting himself and crying out loud, wanted to follow, for Jesus had saved him, had given him back his body, mind, soul. But Jesus said "No." Jesus told him to stay. The people needed a preacher. Life is hell without one. Jesus told him, "Go to your home to your own and spread the message of what the Lord [Jesus—that is, God] has done for you, how he has mercied you" (5:19). The man didn't have to go everywhere Jesus went to follow him, to be a disciple. This is vocation. The man could stay where God had set him. But life did change. He was a follower of Jesus, even as he remained where he was. He'd been preached to and shown mercy. He had been made clean—something he could never have been on his own. God had come from outside of him and made him whole inside and out. He was now the sane man in a land of crazies, people who sent away the Savior. And so he lived, salt and light, set free and firmly planted.

Toe-Tapping and Disruption

Mark 5:21–43

We don't get much of a break here on our race to the cross. When Jesus makes it to the other side of the sea, a great crowd gathered. From the crowd emerged a prominent man, Jairus, a ruler of the synagogue. He made no show. He was a desperate man, at the end of his rope, with no basis for negotiation. His daughter was ill and dying. There was nothing anyone could do . . . except Jesus. And so Jairus threw himself at the Savior's feet, no small thing for a ruler of the synagogue to do. He fell at His feet and confessed. He pleads, "Please come and lay your hands on her to save her" (5:23). There is no indication that this is a hunch, that it might work. Jairus assumes it will work. Come do A so B will result. And Mark simply tells us that Jesus went with him.

Imagine Jairus's hurry. No doubt he wanted to get to his daughter as soon as possible. If there had been an ambulance, he would have been yelling to step on it. Off they headed to save his beloved girl, and what happened? A disruption. Like the guy who won't slow down and get over in traffic when he hears the sirens, someone slowed down the rescue team—namely, Jesus. A woman, a woman also desperate, also at the end of her rope, broke medically, emotionally, and financially, approached Jesus. She didn't speak to him. She wasn't so bold. She had been subject to a flow of blood

for twelve years. She'd gone bankrupt on physicians. They'd
tried everything and only brought her more pain, extra dis-
appointment. But she had an idea. She reached for Jesus' gar-
ment. She said to herself, "If I touch his clothes, I'll be saved"
(5:28). It's not every day you get to lay a hand on God, so she
jumped at her opportunity. And it worked. *Immediately* the
flow of blood dried up. *Immediately* she was healed. All was
good! Imagine her joy.

Jesus could have kept walking. He had a little girl to
save. Jairus was perhaps tugging at His sleeve. But Jesus
stopped. He wanted to talk to the woman, and He wanted
to prove a point to Jairus. He asked, though He knew, giving
the woman a chance to confess, who had touched His clothing. The disciples thought He was crazy. The whole crowd
was touching Him. What did He mean? Didn't he realize
there'd been bodies pressing against Him the whole way. But
she knew what He meant. She knew He was talking to her.
Like a good sermon, preached to a whole congregation, she
heard in His words God's words to *her*. She must have been
terrified. Would she be in trouble? Would He reverse her
healing? Would He charge her? She'd spent all her money.
She didn't even have words to say. She simply came forward
and fell at His feet, her confession of her utter need for His
mercy. She abandoned herself to His compassion. And He
did not chide. He did not lecture. He consoled. He gospeled
her. He sent her away in peace. "Daughter," He said. What
a way to address her! As He stilled the storm, so He stilled
her heart with this greeting. "Daughter," He said, "your
faith has saved you," as faith always does. "Go in peace," He
told her, "healed of your condition" (5:34). And so we find
Jesus in God's service and whenever we dare to throw everything at His pierced feet. Busy with many things, God of
the universe, Upholder of all things, Foundation of truth,
He nevertheless stops for us. We are His disruption, and in
the midst of all the hustle and bustle of all that presses upon

TOE-TAPPING AND DISRUPTION

Him, He calls us to confess, He speaks us peace, He saves, and He heals our affliction. He sends us away whole, having been cleansed and cleansed to remain, through Him, by His power, in His grace.

But what about Jairus? Desperate, frantic, toe-tapping, sleeve-tugging Jairus. Picture him standing there. His daughter's life was ebbing away. This woman could well be the death of her. What was Jesus thinking? Didn't He recognize the urgency? If she died, what good could He be? Now was the time to heal her. But Jesus moves at His own pace, and death must die when He speaks. Jairus needed to chill. He could tap his toes for the next three weeks, and Jesus could still save his daughter if He wanted. And Jesus wanted to save her. He had every intention. She was as good as saved. Jairus needed only to wait.

This was all news to Jairus, though. He wasn't sure how all this Jesus stuff worked. And as his daughter's potential killer distracted the Savior, as the Savior spoke to her *still*, news came. Some from his house arrived and told him, "Your daughter is dead; why bother the teacher anymore?" (5:35). First, it wasn't up to them to decide if he was bothering Jesus. Jesus doesn't get bothered easily, and He would let Jairus know if He was wasting His time. Second, what was this but a hiccup to God? Still, wouldn't your heart have sunk into your stomach if you were Jairus? Can you feel the air leaving your lungs, your life draining from you? And it was at that moment, when Jairus was knee-deep in despair, that Jesus spoke what He speaks to the despairing, without any irony or hint of humor. He spoke a most foolish thing, at least from the perspective of those gathered. Like the friend telling the woman diagnosed with cancer not to worry, Jesus said, "Don't be afraid!" Don't be afraid? Death just swallowed up Jairus's daughter. He'd just lost one of the most precious gifts in his life, he had failed to bring her salvation, he'd let some woman ruin it all, and Jesus tells him not to worry, not to be afraid? "Don't be afraid! Only believe!" (5:36). Notice, as with Levi, Jesus doesn't ask. This is a command. It is a gospel imperative. Believe what? Jesus was standing right there. What more was there to know? "Believe!" Jesus said with a word, and that Word worked what it implored, as it is wont to do with those who have ears to hear, with those at a loss for words whose only recourse is listening.

So they go into the house, and Jesus has more nonsense to tell them. It sure seems like nonsense, that is. He goes into the house, sees the people weeping, causing a big commotion, and in the midst of all this mourning, with the girl dead as dead, He says, "The child isn't dead, she's just sleeping" (5:39). They may have been ancients, and they may not have had iPhones or heated seats, but they weren't stupid. They knew dead when they saw it. And so they did what people still do when God says the dead live, when Jesus speaks life to the deceased. They laughed. The gospel is foolishness to those who are perishing but not to the perished. We are crucified with Christ. We die to live. But this makes no sense to the flesh. They laughed, but Jesus wasn't deterred. A little mockery never kept Him from saving His people. And so He went up to the dead kid (Mark uses such a familiar term for her), took her by the hand, and spoke. "Little girl, I'm talking to you, get up!" (5:41). And she stretched out and yawned and slowly gathered her wits and rolled out of bed. No! *Immediately* she got up. Jesus speaks and it is so. His Word has its way. And He told them to give her some food. Why? Well, she'd been dead. That will take a little out of you, work up an appetite. And just like that, all was good. What a story to tell! But Jesus commanded them, again and again, in various ways, not to tell anyone. He'd not come to be a faith healer, just as He hadn't come to be a bread king. He'd come to suffer and die. He was on a race to the cross. He had to be on His way. And so, after such stern warnings to be silent, He went out.

Jesus' Syrophoenician Dog

Mark 7:24–30

Jesus had just driven home what makes a man unclean and what doesn't, what the chief concern should be. We don't merely wash the outside of a glass. Too many, in the name of religion, had gotten this all backward. They were obsessed with the outward, with the letter of the law, and completely missed the Spirit. They looked at God's commands and thought, "I can do that" and were so confident that they even came up with more. God is clear. The law always accuses, but they had stopped listening. They thought they had a check-list, and they were crossing things off, making their way to heaven one step at a time. But heaven isn't earned; it's given. The law isn't a checklist; it's a death sentence for the sinner. This is why they had no use for Jesus. They simply didn't get it or refused to get it. They were determined to live by the very thing whose ministry was their condemnation, their death.

Someone got it, though. It's no accident that Mark places this account here. He's shaming those whose religion was all too human. Christ came to confound the sociologists, not fit in their categories. The Christian faith is like no other. We do not give to God. God gives to us. We do not get right with Him. He declares us righteous, for the sake of His Son, dead on a tree, victorious from the grave. The law is not a vehicle. It is a death trap for the sinner. We need something more, something else, and not of our creation. We need the Creator, in our flesh, under our curse, dying to put death to death. We need someone to look to, not to put on a show. This is the lesson of the Syrophoenician woman, the Lord's dog. She would rather carefully watch His hands, wait for gifts, even crumbs, and snatch them up like a rambunctious pup, than try to wow him with her person, work, or righteousness.

By all accounts, things did not appear to start well for the woman. Jesus had come into the region and gone into a house in the expressed hope—Mark expresses it—of going unnoticed. Jesus did not want people to know he was there. And yet He was Jesus, and word spread, and somehow this woman found out He was there, and she came to Him, desperate for help, hopeful that He could save her daughter into whom an unclean spirit had entered. Mark makes sure to emphasize here that she was not a Jew. She was Greek (likely not a Jewish convert, that is), a Syrophoenician. The Jesus she encountered didn't seem a friendly one. He did not seem welcoming. He was blunt and seemingly cold. Yet she argued with him. She wasn't going anywhere. He was going to heal her daughter, or at least she was going to do everything in her power to get Him to do so. This woman was special. But Jesus was unmoved: "It isn't right to take the kids food and throw it to the pups"—Mark uses the word for a pup here and not the derogatory term for a dog that the Jews would have used for the Gentiles (7:27). Still, it wasn't an encouraging answer. It bordered on offensive. We might expect the woman to explode or march away at this point, to spread the news about how the so-called Messiah was a bigot and a jerk. And yet that isn't what we see. What happens?

Here's what happens. The woman comes back at Jesus with one of the most beautiful confessions in all of Scripture. She practically leaves Him no option. She confesses, "Lord, even the pups under the table eat the kid's crumbs" (7:28). You've watched children eat. It's not a science. It's an adventure. Food ends up many places besides their mouths. And pups aren't stupid. They know where to post themselves for their spoils. They may be crumbs, scraps, but they are gold for a pup, a true treasure, coveted morsels. That is how the woman viewed any gift from God, from Jesus. His crumbs were more than she deserved, and they were gracious and merciful and good. Even His crumbs were gifts beyond anything the world can give, beyond anything even one's most dearly loved ones here can provide. She was ready to take her post. Her eyes were fixed on God's Child's benevolent hand. Let something fall, Jesus. I'll pounce on it!

Jesus was convinced. "Through this case you've made, go! The demon has already left your daughter" (7:29). More than "it's good as done," Jesus speaks what the gospel always says: "Done." The woman had argued her cause well. She had talked her way into a teachable moment. This unclean, Gentile, irreligious, uncatechized, self-effacing woman proved a model of faith—trust in the mercy of Jesus our Christ, convinced of the power of Jesus' Word. Jesus demonstrated it for all, "Done!" The girl was already healed. The spirit was gone. And when this woman went home, that is precisely what she found, like the disciples on Easter, just as He said.

Spit from God's Own Mouth

Mark 7:31–37

We go now from healing to healing. Sometimes sickness is the result of our own actions, but often it isn't. Often it's the work of Satan, who, as with Job, uses affliction to try to invite doubt into our lives or distract our focus upon Christ, who turns illness into a cross. We mustn't forget that. A bad prognosis isn't necessarily a sign of God's anger. But we are often tempted to think just that, aren't we? It's a very human thought. On the contrary, however, a bad prognosis may well be a sign of God's love for us. It's because God loves us and we, through God's gift of faith, love God, that the devil has a beef with us, after all. We have something he doesn't and can't have—that is, salvation, forgiveness, redemption through Jesus.

It is hard to imagine the life of the deaf man here. Not only was he deaf, but he had a speech impediment. This would seem to imply that he had been deaf from birth, or from a very young age, so that he never learned to speak correctly. It's not easy to be deaf or to deal with a speech impediment in our day, and yet it was far more difficult in Jesus' time. They had none of the resources we have, none of the standardized sign language, warning lights, close captioning, or speech pathologists. Even more, it was a common belief that people were born deaf or mute or blind or became such because of some sin of their parents or of their own. Consider how often he must have examined himself and how that thought must have weighed on his conscience. Maybe you don't have to imagine. Maybe you've been there.

Then what happens? A man named Jesus arrives. Not only a man named Jesus, but a Jew named Jesus. Big whoop, you might think, but it was a big deal. Jesus was in a Gentile region. Gentiles brought this man to the Jewish Messiah. Did they understand the entirety of who He was? Perhaps not. The majority of the Jews didn't. They did realize, however, that He had power from God, that He could heal sickness, another sad consequence of the fall into sin in Eden. And what did Jesus do? He wasn't a very good Jew, was He? At least not in the eyes of many of the religious of His day. He didn't keep His distance from this Gentile. In fact, He took him aside privately; He wasn't putting on a show. He took him aside privately—the first glimmer of promise. He took him aside privately, and He touched him. This happens again and again in Mark's Gospel. Jesus touches the untouchables. Jesus takes hold of those cast off by the church of His day. He could have healed Him from a distance, but He chose to draw near, to make contact.

And now we get to the really interesting part. How did Jesus heal the man? You gotta love it, don't you? He put His fingers into his ears, spit, and touched his tongue—all quite earthy. Keep in mind that the man wasn't blind. What do you think he was thinking as all this took place? When was the last time someone stuck his or her fingers into your ears? Our toddler liked to do that, and it was all right, because she's cute. In fact, one of our sons had to go to the ear, nose, and throat doctor once to get a green bead removed from his ear that she may well have put in there. Has a grown adult stuck his or her fingers in your ears lately, though? Maybe I'll do that next time I preach, when people are leaving church. Rather than shaking hands, I'll stick my fingers in everyone's ears—oh yeah, that and spit. What do you think their reaction would be? Why would Jesus act like this? Why didn't He do something awesome, like the faith healers on TV, like David Copperfield? Wouldn't that have been cooler? That was probably something more along the lines of what the deaf man had imagined. Didn't our Lord have a sense for the spectacular? I guess not. He is earthy as earthy can be.

In the end, I bet the deaf man didn't mind. I'm sure of it, in fact, and I'll tell you why. Jesus charged the man and those who were aware of what happened not to tell anyone what had happened, but what do we read next? They were broadcasting it everywhere. Word quickly spread, and it wasn't that Jesus had done things oddly or grossly but rather that *He had done all things well*. And the more Jesus charged them to be quiet, the louder they got, their zeal only increasing.

Not a bad story, right? It's not every day a deaf man receives his hearing and loses his speech impediment, his tongue loosed. His joy must have been uncontainable. How sweet every voice, every sound we take for granted, must have been in his newly opened ears! And yet that's nothing, nothing at all, compared to what Jesus ultimately came to do and has done.

I want to focus for a moment upon the word Jesus spoke. Do you remember what it was? You can peek. Jesus said, "Ephphatha" (7:34). He sighed—a sign of His emotion, His compassion for those in need, particularly for this man—and then He said, "Ephphatha," which means, "be opened." The same God who created the world with His Word healed His creature with His Word, with a word, "Ephphatha."

Now for an interesting historical tidbit: this word was spoken in the early church's baptismal liturgies. Why would that be? Because a similar thing took place and takes place in Baptism. Think about it. How do we begin Vespers? I chant, "O Lord, open my lips," and then you chant, "And my mouth shall declare Your praise." St. Paul tells us that "faith comes from hearing" and that it is "with the heart one believes and is justified, and with the mouth one confesses and is saved" (Romans 10:17, 10:10). In Baptism and through the preaching and teaching of the gospel, Jesus has spoken to you His *Ephphatha*, has opened your ears as Christians, so that you hear His Word, believe with your heart, and confess with your mouth, your lips opened, your tongue loosed. And this is a miracle far beyond the healing in this Gospel reading, for while the deaf man was healed for this life, you have been healed for all eternity, you will be made whole, not for a few decades, but for ages upon ages. He may not touch your tongue with His spit, but He does with His Body and Blood in, with, and under bread and wine.

Cherish your health. It's a gift of God. When you're ill, turn to your Lord for healing, if it be His will, and for strength to bear up in affliction, to persevere with His promises. Still today, God heals His people's bodies and extends their lives. Consider all the medical advancements, doctors, nurses, and treatments available to you that have been unknown for most of human history and are still unknown throughout much of the world and to the majority of people. Give thanks for that and for every day God gives you here. Do not let your thankfulness end there, though, and do not let your gratitude diminish with your health, should it take a turn for the worse.

You, like the deaf man, have been touched by God. He hasn't spit and touched your tongue, but He's taken hold of you through water, touched your tongue with His Body and Blood. And He hasn't charged you to keep it quiet. Quite the contrary, He's charged us to confess. May our confession be nothing more and nothing less than Christ and Him crucified, who looses the tongues of the mute and gives ears to hear to the deaf.

Less Blind Bit by Bit

Mark 8:22-26

We journey with Jesus again now not far from the shores of the Sea of Galilee, to Bethsaida. Jesus showed up, and it wasn't long before they brought Him a blind man and begged Him to touch him. We understand the expectation. They assumed Jesus touching him would heal him. Indeed, so long as Jesus wanted to heal him, and to heal him in that way, touching him would do it. There was no promise, though. When we have a promise, faith demands, and so the Lord's Prayer is filled with imperatives, with commands. But where there is no promise, there is only pleading. And so they pled, and Jesus listened, and He did touch the blind man. He took hold of the man, and as with other healings, He took him aside, outside the village. He also did something else. You might have guessed it. Yes, He spat again. This time, though, it's even stranger, more stunning: Jesus spat into the man's eyes. As the mute man was not deaf, we are not told that the blind man was deaf or without sensation. This must have been a surprise, something he didn't see coming. Jesus likes to operate like that, doesn't He?

Take note here again that when God makes use of something, even something most ordinary, even something normally rather disgusting, it becomes holy; it becomes a vehicle of His grace and mercy. It remains what it is—in this case, spit—with the supper, bread, and wine (along with His truly present Body and Blood). In our case, we remain ourselves, and yet we also become His, and in all these instances, these common things become a means through which He works His will. Who are we to despise that through which God would work, to recoil or to deign beneath us that which God has deemed fit for His use. No! That thing or person, whatever or whoever he/she/it is, becomes extraordinary, a gift, when God attaches Himself to save, when God takes something or someone up in His hand or places them in ours with a promise.

We might expect the account to get more predictable here. OK, Jesus spit, but now all is good, the man is healed, right? Well, sort of. He regained his sight—some of it. He saw people . . . walking around as trees. This is interesting. Does this mean that the man wasn't born blind, that he had not always been blind? That seems likely. How else would he know what trees look like? Had Jesus failed? Had He underestimated the man's condition? Surely not. So why wasn't the man's sight fully restored? That is a question to ask God in heaven. God doesn't always give us all the details, fill in all the blanks, and there is a lesson in that alone. Perhaps that is why Mark includes these details. Perhaps not. We don't know. It's a helpful reminder, though.

How easily we become impatient with God when He works in stages, don't we? We want Pentecost every Sunday, thousands converted. We want our marriage healed on the spot, our child repentant right this moment, our health restored overnight, one grand conversion attempt that brings only peace of conscience and ease of soul and certainly not crosses. And yet our Jesus sometimes works, for our good and according to His will, in stages, by bits. He doesn't act with play-by-play commentary, explaining every action. He leaves questions to be asked, things about which to wonder. He heals our sight when the Spirit enlightens us with His gifts, when God's grace becomes evident, when we see the pierced hand behind all truth, forgiveness, and life, and yet our understanding also grows in pieces. We see some things dimly, as through a veil; our sight improves as we study the Word, as we hear preaching and are taught. And that is OK, that not everything comes with a snap of the fingers, but in pieces. It's better than OK; it's good and wise, with His goodness and wisdom. And in the meanwhile, we wait. We plead if we have no promise. We demand if we do. And we leave all things to God's direction, even if He spits.

Jesus laid His hands on the man again at this point. Thankfully(?), He didn't spit this time. And the man was healed completely. His sight was fully restored. Now he could see everything as it was. And yet Jesus doesn't do with this man as He does with us when He heals our spiritual blindness. He tells us to go and tell, to spread abroad the glad tidings of His grace. No, Jesus tells the man not to go back into the village. He had a cross to continue toward. While we rejoice in each healing and with those healed, we recognize that He has something even more pressing on the agenda, a greater work to complete: our redemption. The blind man could now see for this life. Jesus was on His way to make sure that blind man and all of us would see the face of God, not for a moment in Bethsaida, but forever.

A Saint's Confession from a Sinner Troubled by the Cross

Mark 8:27-38

Who do people say Jesus is? That's no less a captivating question today than it was when Jesus originally asked it of His disciples. Who do people say Jesus is? You could rattle off a few answers, I'm sure. Watch TV, listen to the radio, surf the web, go to Thanksgiving dinner, talk to some friends in the bar or coffee house. Who is Jesus? There are plenty of answers to that question floating around, some baseless or blasphemous, some true to one degree or another, but disappointingly few hitting upon the heart and center of who Jesus Christ is and what He's done.

Again we venture with Jesus into a Gentile region. Did you realize He spent so much time in such areas, among non-Jews? In fact, this is perhaps the farthest north Jesus ever went, well beyond the comfort zone of many Jews. And yet here we travel with Him on the way to His cross. And here Jesus chooses to ask His disciples that critical question, at the halfway point of Mark's Gospel—this is what Mark's Gospel is after, after all: who Jesus is and what He came to do. Jesus asks, "Who do people say I am?" (8:27). And like us, they had answers. People said all kinds of stuff. People have always had opinions, and many people are eager to share them. They rattle off theories. Some say this, others say that—you know how it goes. But Jesus is after more than that. He gets blunt: "But who do you say I am" (8:29). Peter was quick to answer. As elsewhere, he spoke up for the disciples. We aren't told whether they wanted him to or not, but he did. And this time he did well. He spoke truth. He *confessed*. Peter here speaks for the entire Church—that is, he gives the answer the Church is tasked to give, to *confess*. It's upon this confession that the Church is built. Peter answered, "You are the Christ" (8:29). Jesus is the One, the Messiah, the Savior, He-Who-Saves, our only hope, long promised, now come. Good on Peter! Good for us! This is the heart of the Christian Faith. This is the life of the world. And then Jesus tells them to keep quiet. The cross still loomed. The race must continue. The day would come to go running with this good news, to make it known far and wide, but that was on the other side of Calvary, through an empty tomb.

Peter should have stopped there. But Peter wouldn't have been Peter if he had. Peter was Peter, and it was *that* Peter the Lord would use, all the way to his martyr's death. The Lord loves to use people. Each Evangelist had a writing style. Each apostle had a personality. And so Peter didn't stop there.

Jesus began to speak about His passion. He would suffer many things. He would be rejected . . . by the church. He would be killed. This was not happy stuff. It was dark. It was frightening. After three days, He would rise again, but you had to process all the other stuff before that would sink in. Jesus didn't hold back. Mark tells us that He spoke straightforwardly. This was what was going to happen, matter of fact. And Peter didn't like it. Who would? At this point, we might feel like the pious old saint singing "Were You There?" thinking that he or she would have stopped it. But that would have been a terrible mistake. Great, now everyone goes to hell! No, we would all, if we were there, like it or not, do well to urge Him, "Go, suffer, die." Only in that way are we saved, through His cross and resurrection. That is why He came. That is the point of this race, the ultimate end of this path strewn with sinners.

Nevertheless, Peter didn't like it. It hadn't sunk in. He was still learning, slowly gaining sight like the blind man healed in Bethsaida. He protested. This was a bad idea. There had to be a better way. But his thinking about God, as Luther would later counsel Erasmus, when he objected that the gospel was too much, was too *human* (8:33). God doesn't operate on our terms. Salvation does not come according to our standards. That's why it's a stumbling block. It's not something we could have come up with in a thousand years. God's ways are not our ways; His thoughts aren't ours. Peter had to learn that. He had to keep learning it through prayer, meditation, and temptation all the way to the end when, in agony, Peter was crucified upside down, because, legend says, he considered himself unworthy of a death like his Savior.

Jesus does not call us down an easy path. It is a path to the cross. It is a path through the cross. It is a path marked by crosses. He doesn't hide this from us. He makes it plain:

> If anyone would come after me, let him deny himself and take up his cross and follow me. For whoever would save his life will lose it, but whoever loses his life for my sake and the gospel's will save it. For what does it profit a man to gain the whole world and forfeit his soul? For what can a man give in return for his soul? For whoever is ashamed of me and of my words in this adulterous and sinful generation, of him will the Son of Man also be ashamed when he comes in the glory of his Father with the holy angels. (8:34–38)

The disciples would get one brief glimpse of glory; at least three of them would, including confessing and stumbling Peter. It would be but a glimpse, though. They would yet walk the way of the cross. The Transfiguration follows

in the next chapter. From there, though, the race continues, and throughout it all, Peter's confession must remain
our anchor and life vest, our lens and our remedy. Why?
Because the cross is troubling. As Peter struggled to wrap
His head around it, so also do we. It is a hard message. The
gospel always is. And yet it is certain because it is hard. It is
unshakable. God's promise is true, even in the darkness.
God's Word speaks surely, even when God dies. *He is the
Christ*. That is what we must remember.

The Calm before the Storm

Mark 9:1–13

I'll admit it: I'm going to cheat a little here. Our focus on this journey is upon a path strewn with sinners, indeed, a *race* down it. Here I want us to stop, though. And here I have no sinner for us to ponder, only Christ in His Transfiguration. The three sinners there were called only to watch and listen. We are called to do the same. So I beg your pardon and request your patience. Let's linger briefly at this mount and consider just who it is who has been taking hold of sinners, speaking mercy, and proclaiming grace.

Can this be the same face? Can it possibly be the same face? Can it really be the same face we will behold in weeks to come as we go down this mountain again with Him? Can't we stay here with Him? Can't we stay with Moses, with Elijah? Can't we stay on the mountain? Please, Lord, don't go back down there, to the hatred, to the persecution, to the, you know, what you just told us about before. Lord, don't let this be a reminder, don't let this be a preview; let this be the end, the glorious end. Let us remain here!

Oh, those words had stung at the foot of the mountain! Peter would have none of them. Foolishness, they were pure foolishness! But like a bad song, we can't get them out of our head. The event was tattooed on our brains. Such sour words, such bitter words, which could too often be spoken to us as well, for our thoughts are often human, all too human. "Get behind me, Satan" (8:33), Jesus said. But how could He speak of His cross so sweetly, speak them as if they were the most beautiful words in all the world? Perhaps He spoke them with an air of agony in His voice, and yet was there a glimmer of joy in His eyes. But such words are mere foolishness to us, at least to the flesh. He is the Messiah! Why should He suffer and die? He is the Son of God! Who could possibly overcome Him? The answer is that we could, not by our power, but on account of the power of His love.

Admittedly, this was not the first time Jesus had spoken in such a way, but there was something about this time. There was a sense of immanence, of urgency. He spoke as if it were almost already happening. And then He insisted, He insisted that we go up the mountain with Him, for there was something He wanted us to see.

There is something about God and mountains. Perhaps it is that the climb gives one time to think, to meditate. Perhaps it's that one feels closer to Him on a mountain. Perhaps it's because what God reveals on mountains deserves to be shouted from the mountaintops. There's always been something special about mountains when it comes to God and His people.

Moses climbed a mountain—a terrifying mountain. The people shrank in fear and begged God not to speak to them but to speak only to Moses, for that was a holy mountain, threatening destruction to all who approached it with unclean hands and hearts. God gave Moses the law there, and what a bloody law it was, so full of threats and blood and death! It was serious business. God gave it to be fulfilled. Taking a stab at fulfilling it was not enough. Good intentions were not enough. God gave it to be fulfilled, but thus far, everyone had fallen dreadfully short.

Elijah climbed a mountain; he climbed a mountain for battle. Almost all of Israel had fallen from the Faith.

They bowed to statues of stone and wood. They offered what belonged to God to demons dressed as gods. They persecuted the prophets and ridiculed the remnant. So God told Elijah to climb that mountain and do battle. And Elijah did. He preached against the priests of Baal, against the idolatry of God's people, and in His grace and love, God gave Elijah victory, proving with fire and blood that He was the only true God, the God who crushes with the law, but also the God who beckons back His wayward children with good news of forgiveness, of deliverance.

Moses climbed the mountain to receive the law. Elijah climbed the mountain to proclaim God's Word. And those mountains, the Law and the Prophets, made up the Old Testament. And now Jesus has invited us up a mountain . . . where we will meet both of them, Moses and Elijah. Here the Law and Prophets meet, the veil is lifted, and where before they had known only a coming Messiah through shadows and symbols, Moses and Elijah now meet Jesus face to face, the arrived Messiah, who shines with a radiance the world has never known, with the light of a thousand promises burning in one flame of fulfillment. This day is what had refreshed them in their tiresome labor, what lifted them up when everything else weighed them down. And now, with dazzling brilliance, Moses and Elijah meet on a new mountain, a better mountain, and see in all His splendor the one whom they foretold, proclaimed, promised so long ago. Oh, if we could only stay on this mountain! It was no surprise that Peter couldn't help but say as much, to suggest a building project to celebrate this moment.

And for once, Jesus didn't have to tell Peter to be quiet. A cloud appeared and the Father spoke: "This is my Son. I love him. Listen to him!" (9:7). What a glorious day this was! The Son shines, the Father speaks! What could ever be more important than this? But, alas, this was not the finale; the most glorious day would instead be the goriest. This was an encouragement as the end yet approached, as the end awaited just down this mountain. The Father had spoken His approval at Jesus' Baptism, as He began His earthly ministry, and now He speaks it as His earthly ministry approaches its disturbing end. As quickly as that, plain old Jesus is back again. Drunk as Peter and the others had been with delight at the sight of His transfigured glory, at their glimpse at His seemingly all-too-often hidden divinity, this was a hot cup of coffee, sobering and saddening. Plain old Jesus is back and bidding us down the mountain.

Could that have been the same face? Could that possibly have been the same face? Could that really have been the same face that is now resolutely set on Jerusalem, on another mountain, on Calvary? Don't forget that face, because that is who suffers for you down the path, who takes resolute step after resolute step to your punishment, to your death, to your tomb. Remember that face, the face of the One who brings Moses and Elijah together on the same mountain and fulfills the Law and the Prophets, the One whom the Father loves. Remember that face and see your own face in it, for His coming death is your death to sin, and His coming resurrection is your resurrection to a new life in Him, begun now, and realized in all its resplendent glory when you will rise to shine like that face set before us on this mountain. It's the same face.

I Do Believe; Help My Unbelief!

Mark 9:14–29

When Jesus returned to His disciples, they were in the middle of quite the commotion. He asked what was going on, and a man answered plainly. He had brought his son for the disciples to heal him. The son had an unclean spirit. He was in a very bad way. This spirit was extremely destructive. In the spirit's control, the boy was mute, foamed from the mouth, ground his teeth, and became rigid. The father was desperate, and the disciples were unable to help.

Jesus appears frustrated and asks how long He has to bear with such a faithless generation. He tells them to bring the boy to Him. He seems bothered by it all. As when the disciples thought He was sleeping in the boat, apparently they had wavered in His absence when this boy was brought to them. When they brought Him the boy, the spirit immediately overcame him. He dropped and flopped, convulsing and foaming at the mouth. Like a good physician, Jesus asked how long this had been happening. Too long, no doubt, in the father's estimation. It had been happening since childhood, he told Jesus. As always, the devil had been destructive. The boy had often thrown himself into water and into fire.

Imagine how helpless the father had felt all those years. Fathers are supposed to protect their children. Those of us who are fathers know how guilty we can feel when something happens to our children, even when it isn't our fault. This father had been through the grinder. He had no pretense or pride. This father wasn't here to negotiate. He was here to beg. He appealed to Jesus' compassion—never a bad strategy! He pleads for mercy. "If you can do anything," he says (9:23). And Jesus caught his words and jumped on them. "'If you can'?" Jesus scolds. "Everything is possible for those who believe." Of course Jesus could heal the boy if He wanted. His ability wasn't at issue. It wasn't a matter of "can" but "will." Would Jesus heal him? That was what was up in the air.

Here I can't help but love this man. These words from Jesus could have snuffed out what little remained of any of his faith. But he persisted. He was so desperate, he couldn't afford not to believe. He wasn't going to pretend. He wasn't going to put on a show. He wasn't a poster boy, and he didn't intend to be. What little faith there is in him cries out. "I do believe," he confesses. But he isn't done. He adds, "Help my unbelief!" (9:24). And we hear no more from Jesus. He rebukes the spirit. He casts it out. He answers the poor father's prayer. His weak faith was faith, and that weak faith received that for which it asked. The boy convulsed terribly. Many thought he had died. It often looks that way when the devil is cast out. It indeed is that way when the devil is cast out. We die to sin. We are buried with Christ, crucified with Him. We rise to a new life in Him. And so did this boy. He was healed. He was given back to his father whole and new. Jesus took him by the hand, helped him up, and gave him to his old man, whose hairs likely bore their fair share of gray from all the heartache and anguish his son's long plight had caused him. I often thought of this account when I served in the parish, when I gave a child back to their parents after Baptism. The devil had been renounced, cast out. The old Adam had been drowned. The child now had a new Father. Jesus had given life. Weak faith or strong faith, their parents' prayers were answered.

Many of us can identify with the father in this story. When pressed, our faith has often waivered. It has been less strong than we ever thought it could be, perhaps. Doubts shot through our mind. Our heart grew heavy and cold. God's promises became but a distant echo of what they had been before in our ears. The Scriptures took on the air of platitudes. God seemed unconcerned. We felt helpless—indeed, we were! And yet Jesus is stubborn, even when He is stern. He bears with us. He rebukes whatever spirits torment. Perhaps there is no immediate, emotional relief. Perhaps the trial continues. But He is there. Maybe He chips away. Maybe He does grant immediate relief. Either way, it's not that we have believed so well. It is that He has been so faithful. His promises don't become untrue because we doubt them. He is not far away just because He doesn't seem near. Into the commotion, He comes with His Word, and that Word refuses to let go of us. That doesn't make everything better in the moment. That doesn't make everything easy. It isn't always neat and clean. It is often muddy, foamy, a whirl of commotion. And sometimes we don't even realize that the Word is at work. But it is. And so we pray, we plead, we maybe even cry out, "I do believe. Help my unbelief!" And He does. And He will. He is greater than our hearts. He does not lie. He does not let go of even one of those entrusted to His care. He is our Jesus. Should we doubt it, we need only look down the path and consider where He runs. It is no coincidence that the next thing He speaks about is His passion. Tiring as this faithless generation might have been, taxing as the all too often weak faith of His disciples and those who approached Him for help might have been, He was still resolute, determined as ever to be on His way.

Let the Little Sinners Come to Me

Mark 10:13–16

What a compelling and yet tender glimpse of Jesus we get on our next stop. People were bringing their children to Jesus for Him to touch them. This was a rather natural thing. What parent in their right mind wouldn't want God to bless their little one? People were bringing their children to Jesus for Him to touch them, and His disciples rebuked them. Why? They were functional Baptists. They didn't understand the nature of faith. They also thought it was a waste of Jesus' time. But Jesus had no patience for such thinking. He turned everything on its head. He rebuked the ones who had been rebuking. He commands the very thing they had been trying to forbid. He said, "Let the little children come to me. Don't stop them. The kingdom of God belongs to this sort" (10:14). Even more, He explained, "Anyone who won't receive the kingdom of God like a child won't enter it" (10:15). Talk about toppling manmade religion and human philosophy. You want to be saved? Be like a child. And not just a child but, as we know from the Gospels as a whole, a *little* child.

What is Jesus after here? He's teaching us what faith is. Faith isn't primarily memorizing and regurgitating facts. It isn't a journey of self-discovery and personal growth. It isn't hard-earned nuance. It isn't anything people easily make it out to be. It is trust. It is trust planted within us. It is the trust a child has for his or her parents.

Do you remember when you were born? Do you remember when the doctor said, "This is your mother. She is this tall and weighs this much. She is from this place. She likes this and doesn't like that"? Do you remember that? Of course you don't. You knew Mom. It was planted in you. And you trusted her. You stopped crying when placed upon her chest. Mom was Mom, and although you couldn't articulate why in any great detail—indeed, not at all—you knew she would protect you. You even laughed if she tossed you in the air. You trust was rooted entirely in Mom. She was good and gracious and wise. She opened her hand and provided good things. That was faith. That is the nature of faith in God. You were dependent. Mom was good. We are dependent. God is good. We are set free by such trust. We are saved by it—faith planted in us by God Himself through Word and Sacrament. We are born again, not by human decision, not by the will of a father or mother, but by grace, through water and the word, and we trust, as we trusted Mom, as children of God, as those who trust His love, even when we can't perfectly articulate it in every situation and at every time. And so we bring the little sinners to Jesus. We baptize the little wretches, for to such belongs the kingdom of God. And in the process, we learn something.

When we baptize infants, they don't walk to the font. They don't ask for Baptism. They don't speak at all, and in fact, often they cry and protest. Nevertheless, God takes hold of them, and they trust with a trust that only gets more strained as we age, as we get more jaded and brittle in a world full of broken promises. We can learn from them, then, as they rejoice in God's person and promise, as nothing is more plain than His love, demonstrated by the cross and tomb of which they so often gladly and loudly sing, if not in the right key. And as we grow in knowledge and wisdom, as the Christ

Child Himself did, I pray God in His goodness will provide ample opportunities for us to be reminded of just what faith is, and what it isn't, so that we grow, not up toward heaven, as if we would ascend there ourselves by our thoughts or works, but deeper into the water of our Baptism and adoption as sons and daughters. Jesus drives that home as we next encounter a man who thinks he has done the math; who thinks he is climbing the ladder, walking the walk, working his way to God; and who needs not to grow up but to grow down, to trust more and toil less.

An Epic Fail

Mark 10:17-27

"Good Teacher," the man says (10:17). That's a respectful way to address the Lord, isn't it? So why does Jesus seem so bothered by it? I suppose part of it is that we ought not toss about titles lightly, especially in the Church. Jesus wants this rich young ruler to understand the implications of his words. Jesus was, Jesus is, the "Good Teacher," having the words of everlasting life. He's the "Good Teacher," not simply because He has a rabbi's gift for teaching, but because He alone is good—that is, He is God made manifest among us.

The rich young ruler knelt before Jesus in a servant's pose. In this way, he was closer to the kingdom than many, especially those Pharisees who had seen in Christ someone below them and their counterfeit righteousness. He's in the right pose before the right Person, but he's still not quite there, as his question will demonstrate.

"What must I do to inherit eternal life?" (10:17). He ran to Christ like the lame and leprous, but not to be healed. He wanted to learn to heal himself. He wanted advice, not death and resurrection. So Jesus must bring the kneeling to his knees, showing him the end of this road we call work-righteousness, the notion we do anything to earn what God gives only as a gift. What is the end of the road? It's despair, and the very fact that this rich young ruler was already desperate enough to consult a poor young itinerant Rabbi condemned by the experts shows us that he was partway down that road to begin with.

So what was the prescription for the man's reliance upon the law? More law. Jesus wields the law, smacks him upside the head with it, to teach him the law's limits, what it just can't do. Jesus is like a father letting his child gorge on candy to teach them what happens when you gorge on candy: "You know the commandments" (10:19). But notice Jesus only lists the commandments from the second table of the law, those that deal with our relationship with our neighbor. And even then, Jesus leaves off the last two commandments, which pry into the thoughts and attitudes of the heart, unseen by men but plain as day to God, to the "Good Teacher."

"Teacher"—he leaves off the "Good" this time—"I've been doing all that since I was young," the young man replies (10:20). To Lutheran ears, that is a pretty cocky reply. And yet what do we read? "Jesus loved him." Wow! Why? Not because the man was perfect, but because he was sincere. He wanted to go to heaven. He wanted to be right with God. He'd taken the law seriously, as God would have us take it. Tragically, however, he did not yet understand the purpose of the law, which is to herd us, like wandering sheep, into the pen of the gospel. Precisely because He loves this young man, Jesus must drive him to helplessness so that he'll be willing to receive help, crushing him with the very law by which he wants to be saved. And so Jesus lovingly wields the First Commandment like a club, to knock theological sense into this young man. Maybe he'd kept the second table of the law, at least the Fourth through Eighth Commandments, and at least according to the letter, if not the spirit, but his heart was not as clean as his rap sheet. He did not yet fear, love, and trust in God above all things.

Now here we must cast aside the confusion that often arises at this point. Jesus doesn't now condemn riches, and He doesn't give a universal command to sell one's riches to be saved. People make the very same mistake the young man was making—looking to the law for something only the gospel can give—when they latch onto Jesus' words in such a way. Jesus, looking into this man's heart, speaks to this man and cuts to the heart of the matter. This man had made his riches his treasure and, in that way, another god. God's material gifts to this man had been turned into spiritual hindrances. That was the problem. He thought he'd been keeping the commandments, but he hadn't even gotten past the first, he *couldn't* even make it past the first. He didn't need a nudge in the right direction or a shot in the arm. He needed to die to himself. He needed to despair, not of God, but of his works, and then, like a child, confess his utter dependence, his *need* for salvation, and not merely his *desire* to inherit eternal life.

"Where is your treasure?" Jesus asks. "Is it standing before you, or is it behind you, in your home, your barn, your purse? You cannot set your eyes, let alone your heart, on both at once." As Jesus was wont to say, "Where your treasure is, there your heart will be also" (Matthew 6:21, Luke 12:34). The man's reaction answers the question. He turns back and walks farther down the road to despair, the end of the road we call work-righteousness. And unfortunately, the disciples don't seem to be far behind him.

"Who then can be saved?" (10:26). That's a great question. It should be everyone's question all the time. When even the most religious fall short, when even our best days—the days we keep the second table pretty darn well—prove to be a sham, who can be saved? If this very devout young man who runs to Jesus with zeal and kneels before Him in humility can't do it, who can? If the rich are damned, what hope is there for the poor? And don't we often think this way? We see God's blessing in abundance and His curse in affliction.

We assume the so-called good times are the godly times. But that is not God's logic at work. That is our fallen reason. How quickly we forget that the empty tomb followed an occupied cross, that our greatest Treasure rested in a manger, that the martyrs lost their heads to win a crown!

Following that crucified Treasure does promise the glory of an empty tomb, but that tomb is found on the other side of the cross. "Take up your cross and follow me," the Savior invites us. Sometimes the sweetest gift of God is the most bitter pill, as He kills in us everything that would turn our eyes from "His holy, precious blood and . . . his innocent suffering and death" to the hollow riches and counterfeit peace that the Devil would use to distract us, just as He tried to do with Christ in the desert. How much more splendid is Christ's poverty compared to the devil's plenty!

After Luther's death, the Roman Catholic emperor marched through Germany to make the Lutheran lands subject to the papacy again. He succeeded in capturing the Elector of Saxony, Luther's former protector, John Frederick—not a man renowned by his piety, although certainly known for his confession. John Frederick was robbed of his lands, his title, and his dignity. Still, he would not trade the gospel for all that he had lost. Angry, the Emperor ordered that John Frederick also be robbed of his books, including Luther's writings and, most importantly, his German Bible. John Frederick responded, "The books one can very well take from me; however what I have learned from them, one cannot tear out of my heart." In John Frederick's poverty, Christ was his treasure.

Receive Christ's poverty as the very priceless riches of heaven. Take the treasure He has dearly purchased for you and make it your own. Salvation is standing before you. Salvation is Jesus Christ. You cannot do salvation; you can only receive salvation. Salvation is a gift from God, not a gift to Him. Salvation is God made man, not man made God. You have not found salvation, though you have sought it. Salvation has found you, because He sought you. And having been found, turning from Him can bring nothing but sorrow and despair.

To love God is to be loved by God. To love God is to call what He calls good and to receive what He gives for good as a priceless treasure, even when what He gives for good doesn't sparkle or shine as we'd prefer. The rich young man went away rich, but sorrowful. Today, whether there's cash in your wallet or cattle in your barn, you can go away rich and joyous, for your Jesus is your Treasure, sold for thirty coins of silver to "purchase and win you from all sins, from death and from the power of the devil,"[2] having left behind the treasures of heaven to pursue you as His treasure. His poverty is your abundance, and His cross is your glory. Better a cross from the Good Teacher than a thousand kingdoms from the wicked foe. Better a heaven begged than a hell earned. Better a penny lost for the Savior's sake than an eternity lost for our own.

---

[2]"Redemption," *Luther's Small Catechism*, http://catechism.cph.org/en/creed.html.

A Roadside Beggar

Mark 10:46–52

If anyone was prepared for his encounter with Jesus, it was blind Bartimaeus. He was a beggar. He was a roadside beggar. He'd long ago cast off shame. He was out in the open, in need, without airs, humbled by the hardships of life in a fallen world. Luther died with a confession that we are beggars all—and Bartimaeus was a professional. And so when Jesus left Jericho and a great crowd followed and someone explained that all the to-do was about Jesus of Nazareth, Bartimaeus didn't hesitate. He didn't try to come up with clever words. He didn't try to craft some pious promises. He began to cry out, and what He cried out is one of the most beautiful prayers in all of Scripture. He confessed and beseeched all in one sentence. He shouted, "Jesus, Son of David, have mercy on me!" (10:47). Short and sweet, precocious and powerful. He told Jesus who He was—that is part and parcel of giving Him right praise—and He asked Jesus for what Jesus came to bring, that is, mercy. He asked the right person for the right thing, and he did so as a beggar. And he did so over and over again, even when others told him to give up and get out, when they rebuked him and told him to shut up. He had his prayer, and he had a promise. No, God didn't have to heal him, but God did *have* to show him mercy. God had promised as much. And so Bartimaeus refused to be quiet. He confessed and begged, and Jesus picked up the ball and ran with it.

Have you noticed how often Mark has driven home this aspect of Jesus' ministry? The outcast, the undesirables, the clearly, plainly, openly, no-way-to-hide-it afflicted come to Jesus, and where others see a waste of time or unworthiness, Jesus is moved to compassion. The unworthies come or cry out, from children to lepers to roadside beggars, and Jesus hears, not noise, not annoyance, but the prayer of the faithful, even when they feel faithless, like the man who prayed for help with his unbelief. Jesus let the back-and-forth between those with him and Bartimaeus play out for a while, but then He stopped. He summoned the blind man. His disciples called him over, telling him to "take heart" (10:49). The fact was, he had already taken heart. He had seized the moment long before Jesus called to him. He knew who Jesus was and what He came to bring. He cast off his cloak, jumped to his feet—imagine that sight—and hustled to the Savior.

Here Jesus asked an odd question. Jesus said, "What would you like me to do for you?" (10:51). The man had already answered what he wanted. He wanted mercy. Jesus now asks what the blind man wants him to do. It was obvious, and yet Jesus gives this beggar the privilege of asking, on his feet, looking God in the eye, as a person and not an annoyance, as the outcast turned the Savior's friend. God stopped everything and gave him his moment. And so Bartimaeus spoke up, "Rabbi, I want to see again" (10:51). Bartimaeus already had mercy. The incarnate Christ was hanging on his words. Now was his chance to receive a lesser gift too. And Jesus reply was simple: "Go on and get out of here; your faith has made you well" (10:52). I am translating a little freely, of course, but Jesus' point is clear: "Done!" Why? The man trusted. Even more, he trusted the right person: Jesus! It was not the strength of Bartimaeus's faith that brought healing; it was the strength of Jesus' healing. It wasn't the beggar's hand; it was what it held. It wasn't the power of his words. It was the power of Jesus' words, of His promise. The merciful show mercy. Bartimaeus was unwilling to let that go; he was stubborn in the promise and person of Christ. And this is how we head into Palm Sunday, with a reminder of who Jesus is, what He has come to bring, and what we do well to beg, and even demand, of Him.

The Oh-So-Close Scribe

Mark 12:28–35

We've made quite the jump now. We've rushed headlong through Palm Sunday and into Holy Week. Along that way, as we tumble toward Calvary, we meet a scribe. He's not quite there yet, at the cross, in the gospel, but he's inching closer. He's listening. He's thinking. He's not turning his back on Jesus. In fact, he thinks *Jesus* is onto something. He's opening up to Him as a teacher. And that's good. Jesus is a teacher. But He is also so much more. He is the Savior, *the scribe's* Savior, and that is what the Spirit is working on the scribe to see.

The scene develops in a really natural way. The religious elite were disputing with Jesus, as they were wont to do. The scribe stumbled upon the discussion. Like a guy at the bar overhearing an interesting conversation and jumping in, the scribe did the same. He noticed that Jesus answered his opponents well and wanted to learn more. He asked Jesus, it seems entirely sincerely, "Which commandment is most important?" (12:28). This is the sort of question one might expect from a scribe. Many a great teacher had wrestled with it. The scribe wanted *Jesus'* answer, and not to attack him, but to learn. He was like the man in church who might not quite believe yet but still comes to church every week to listen. He is curious. He is interested. He is *listening*. And that is how God catches people, isn't it, through the ears? While we certainly want everyone to believe, to be convinced fully of the person and work of Christ, we do still have to rejoice when they at least listen. They've not closed the door. The Spirit is at work. God's promises are being heard—at least I hope so, if the pastor isn't on his bully pulpit or preaching a sermon series on some tripe.

Jesus, recognizing the sincerity of the scribe, didn't hesitate to answer. And, as Jesus was accustomed to do, He answered well. That Jesus, he really knew theology! Jesus broke it down simply. The greatest commandment is to confess and love God. Jesus even cited the Old Testament creed as part of his answer. The second commandment is similar. Love God by loving your neighbor. Jesus made this point elsewhere when He told the sheep and the goats that whatever they did for the least they did for Him.

In response to Jesus' good answer, the scribe gave a pretty good answer. God is One, and loving God is the main thing. In fact, loving God was better than sacrifice and the other works of the law. Loving God was *the* thing. Everything flowed from that. And it does. The question is, How do we love God when we are born at enmity with Him? How do we love Him *enough?* John would later make the answer clear in his letters. We love God, not so that He loves us, but *because* He loves us. As Luther put it in the Heidelberg Disputation, God does not find those who love Him and then love them; no, He finds the unlovable and loves them. As a result, the unlovable can't help but love. They can't help but love Him who so loved them without any grounds or reason, with nothing in return, and they can't help but love those He also loves, our neighbor. Now, for sure, this love for God and for neighbor is imperfect in this life. We stumble and waver; we too often hope for reciprocity and show affection only begrudgingly, and yet it is love—love worked by God's love for us. In short, love breeds love.

Jesus saw that the scribe answered well, thoughtfully, open to correction, and replied, "You are not far from the

kingdom of God" (12:34). The scribe was close. He was hon-
estly considering the law. He was pondering the words of
God. What he needed now was to weigh himself according
to the entirety of God's law, to recognize he could not keep it
perfectly, to realize that salvation was unattainable according to its standards. I do not doubt the scribe loved God, but
his love, as Kierkegaard once noted, was ultimately a love for
himself. He loved a God who loved him because he loved
God. What he lacked was trust. He was unwilling to let go
and let himself fall into the pierced hands of the crucified
alone for rescue. He was still in the mode of working on it.
He was chipping away at the law, crossing things off, doing
his best. What he needed to realize was that his best was
not good enough and that we don't chip away at the law, but
rather it cuts us to pieces. The scribe needed the gospel, he
needed to abandon himself with nothing more than the rad-
ical grace of Christ, which alone is enough, through which
alone heaven is attainable, not by our works, but by those of
the Savior.

And what do we hear from Mark next? "No one dared
to ask him more questions after that" (12:34). Why? This
man had spoken well. This man was religious. This man was
trying. He was listening. He was sincere. And yet he wasn't
there. He was "not far," but he also was still falling short. As
when the rich young man went away dejected, so also now,
some wondered, "If he can't do it, who can? If he's not there
yet, can anyone get there?" The answers were, of course, "He
can't" and "No one can." That needed to sink in, though. I
like to think that it eventually did, that this scribe was later
numbered among the disciples. I don't know that he for sure
ever got there, but he was on his way, not by doing more, but
by listening, by having salvation done to him, through the
preaching and teaching of Jesus the Christ, and not by him.
From here, Jesus continued His way to the cross. I pray that
the scribe eventually ended up there too.

Anointing the Anointed for Death

Mark 14:3-9

Jesus' death is quickly approaching. The race is nearing its end. And yet Jesus finds time for the outcast again. He's in Bethany, not far from Jerusalem, the hometown of Lazarus, Mary, and Martha. He isn't at their house, though. He's reclining in the house of Simon the Leper. How's that for a nickname? Obviously, this man was no longer afflicted, but he still was known for likely the worst part of his life. He'd been a leper. He'd been cast off from society. He'd been unclean. And now he's still known for it, although the title perhaps brought him joy, reminded him of that from which he'd been delivered. Had Jesus healed him? We're not told, but it seems likely. Anyway, we find ourselves in Simon's house with Jesus next in our Holy Week journey. Is that where you would expect to find Jesus in this week of the passion? And yet is there perhaps a more predictable place for Him to be?

Into Simon's house came, perhaps sneaked, a woman. She brought an alabaster jar of pure nard, an expensive ointment. And what did she do with it? She poured it over Jesus' head. This is interesting. This isn't like when a young man says something offensive to a young lady and she exacts her revenge with her ice water, but it is out of the ordinary. It struck those around Jesus. Unfortunately, it struck them the wrong way. Some became indignant. This woman had done a beautiful thing; she humbly gave Jesus her best, with a very physical prayer, although in a bit of a surprise attack, and right over the noggin. Nevertheless, she took *her* perfume and anointed Christ. She hadn't stolen it. It was hers to do as she saw fit. But they chided her. She could have sold it and given to the poor—and couldn't we always with every nice thing we have?

Jesus would not scold her, though. First, while Jesus clearly wants us to help those in need, we will always have the poor. There will be no utopia. We need not worry the poor will vanish and with them our opportunity to serve. Second, the woman's action confessed something. She was preparing Jesus for His burial. While the apostles had been slow to listen and quick to forget, she was getting Jesus ready for the homestretch of His race to the cross and for His rest in another's tomb. We certainly have Jesus today in Word and Sacrament, even with His true Body and Blood, but we do not have Him as this woman and those gathered in the leper's house did. He would only be present in that way for so much longer. The woman anointed, confessed, while she had yet time. And so what does Jesus tell us? "Wherever the gospel is preached in the entire world, people will talk about what she did" (14:9). And here we are. But notice the connection. Her action confessed the gospel. It pointed to the death and burial of the Messiah. It was a stunning act of love by one loved by God, for whom God would give His life, for whom He would rest in the grave. Ultimately, that is the most beautiful thing we can do too, to confess Jesus as He is, the One crucified for sinners, and to see in that a love worthy of our best and infinitely more. She anointed the anointed because He was doing what the anointed was promised to do. He was running His race to completion; He was hurrying to His cross and Joseph's tomb, into which He was placed for our forgiveness, out of which He would walk for our justification.

God's Supper with Sinners

Mark 14:12-25

God's people had been in slavery for generations, and the slavery grew crueler and more unbearable every year. Many had given up any hope of deliverance. Even when a prophet came promising it, many laughed it off. They were slaves. That was their life. That was what it had been. That was what it would be. And then one day, that deliverance became concrete (not that the earlier plagues had been anything to blink at). Israelite families took a lamb, their best lamb, perfect, without blemish. They slit its throat and drained its blood. They marked their doorposts with that blood, so that death would pass over. They cooked the lamb and ate it. They partook of the sacrifice that brought their deliverance.

"Where do you want us to go to prepare the Passover for you to eat it?" Jesus' disciples asked Him (14:12). He gave clear instructions, amazingly clear. He sent two disciples. He told them to go into the city and find a man carrying a jar of water. In fact, this man would meet them. They were to say something to him that certainly must have seemed odd when Jesus told them: "The Teacher says, Where is my guest room?" (14:14). How was this guy supposed to know that? Wouldn't he look at them like fools? Jesus then added, "He'll show you a big upper room, with furniture, ready to go" (14:15).

God was in control. This was His Passover. It was important. Everything would be as it should.

As they reclined at the table and ate, Jesus told them one of them would betray Him. Talk about hard words to speak. And yet one of them would, and Jesus didn't hide the fact. He knew it would happen. He let them know. And how did they reply? Oh, how this cuts to the heart! "Is it me?" they asked Him, one after the other (14:19). Why did they ask? They weren't sure. They knew what lurked within them. They weren't naïve. Their flesh hung around their neck. It was inescapable. And so they asked, "Me?" And can't you identify with them? We know what we are capable of doing, saying, and thinking. We know what lurks within us. Our flesh hangs around our neck. Try as we might, even on our good days, we are capable of unspeakable evil. Thank God, we usually manage to avoid some of it, but it is there, the possibility, the potential. Even at our most devout, the old Adam pulls at our heartstrings, we are a thought away from disaster, from everything caving in. There have been countless close calls. Oh, if people only knew what we've carefully hidden, sometimes for decades! Eleven of them would not betray Him, at least not at Judas did. Yet all but John would flee. Peter would deny Him. Thomas would doubt His resurrection. None of them would come out unscathed. The question makes sense. It is our question too. "Is it me?"

Here Jesus celebrated His Passover and prepared to die the next day, and what surrounds Him? Sinners. Sinners, the whole lot. And yet Jesus doesn't stomp out. He doesn't get flustered. He doesn't decide to change His plans or quit the race. He looks out on these faces so unsure of their love for Him and gives them one of the greatest gifts ever given: He institutes a family. He celebrates a supper for sinners. In the midst of all the darkness of this trial, He gives them Himself. He gives them the very Body and Blood that would hang on the tree. He gives it to the Church of all ages. Here sinners find the food of saints. Here we find medicine for our frailty, food for our faith, and inoculation against doubt, and not in some magical way, or bit by bit, or as a steroid to help us work harder, but in the same way that He first came to us in Baptism or through preaching, with His promise, with His Word, here connected with bread and wine.

Christians can and have debated the exact nature of the Lord's Supper until they are blue in the face. Christ did not give it as a subject of speculation, though. He did not give it as a doctrine, though there is certainly a doctrine of the Lord's Supper. He gave it as a means *for the forgiveness of sins*. He gave it *for you*. He gave it *for me*. Here Christ comes to us, even as He sat there with His apostles. Here He comes, even better, the crucified and risen, having finished His race, now setting before us, placing into our mouths by the hands of a called servant, the benefits of all that He has done. Here He shares His crown; He gives us a taste of victory. Here the saints gather on both sides of the altar to rejoice in that which makes them who they are: Jesus Christ, the friend of sinners. Anything that detracts from that, from the simple fact that Christ truly comes in the Sacrament to feed me with His grace, having called me to His table through Baptism and the Word, as part of His family, cannot be anything but false teaching and a denial of the full breadth and power of the gospel. The Christ we find at the altar is the same Christ we've journeyed with so far. He is that Christ or no Christ. He is not an idea. He is a person. He is promise wrapped in bread and wine. He is God made man *for me* and *for you*. He is Mark's odd, persistent, preaching, reaching, touching, sitting with sinners and outcasts Jesus in full force and with free forgiveness, completely unasked and unearned, as a gift and in no other way. As in Baptism, we are only recipients. We bring only sinful mouths and hands. We come on sinful feet. He is the Host. He is the Active One. He is the Giver. And we should not want it, and we cannot have it, at least not as He has established it, in any other way.

The Passion Streaker

Mark 14:51–52

Here I'm going to assume a little liberty. I cannot prove the young man who fled Jesus' arrest naked is Mark. However, plenty of very capable and respectable scholars have my back on this one, as well as pretty solid church tradition. So we'll roll with it. In no way does it detract from the gospel or Christian doctrine. It does fit very well with the narrative and themes of Mark. This young man fits right in with the other sinners we've met along the path, and it makes perfect sense that, if Mark was the man who fled naked, as I am pretty convinced he was, he would include it, in keeping with his emphasis upon the love of Christ for sinners, for those who come to him marked by frailty, failure, and a lack of faith.

Why was Mark there? Different scholars have different ideas. Some argue that when Mark heard what was happening, he rushed there from home, wearing only this linen cloth. Whatever the case, Mark seems to place himself smack dab in Gethsemane, and not at his best. He is the passion streaker. He flees naked, frightened, confused. Some have speculated that Mark did this as a distraction, to help Jesus, to draw the attention of his captors, but I'm not sure I buy it, interesting as it might be. Either way, Mark puts himself there—or at least he sure seems to put himself there—and the Mark we find isn't the stuff of illustrated Bibles or Sunday School books.

Why would Mark do that? Why even include it if the young man isn't Mark? Why not leave it out? Why paint himself in such a way for his readers? I think it's not that hard to figure out why. This is how we all find ourselves before Jesus, especially at our lowest, especially in our dark Gethsemanes. Naked Job came from his mother's womb, and naked he would depart, and ultimately, naked we stand before our God unless He dresses us. This same Mark who fled, who streaked the passion, would go on to write one of the most important and influential books in all of human history. He would, after some homesickness, become a renowned missionary. The Good News marked and defined his life. Whatever he was, even a passion streaker, He is God's child and ever will remain the same. Christ has clothed him in rich array, beyond anything this world can produce. He has dressed him in a robe of righteousness, Jesus' own righteousness declared Mark's, put upon Him in Baptism, laundered daily through the Resurrected's Absolution.

Does the devil ever try to keep you from God precisely with the notion that God might see your shame and no longer love you, that God might turn His face and look upon you no more? Nonsense. The devil is a dolt and a liar. God has seen your shame, long before you ever thought to confess it. He has seen your nakedness, and far from it driving you from His heart, it has endeared Him to you, it has pulled His Son from heaven to dress you as His Bride, to make you a delight. Never forget that. Whether this passion streaker was Mark or not, that is and will remain true: God is shameless in His love for the shameful. That is *the* truth the Truth was made man to make it clear. Hold to it, even if you should find yourself naked, confused, frightened, and in the darkest night.

Oh, and I'm pretty sure the young man was Mark.

Peter Denies Jesus

Mark 14:66–72

As mentioned in the introduction, the common view is that Mark's Gospel was heavily influenced by Peter. If so, and I am pretty darn sure it is, then we have another layer here. Peter would no doubt have struggled to retell this part of his life and the Lord's passion. This was a very bumpy part of the path to the cross. This was where Peter fell during the race to Calvary, and fell hard. Many probably didn't expect him to recover. Having committed three years to following Jesus, what he did at this moment must have seemed insurmountable. How could he get past having acted so coldly, so cowardly, so hurtfully against the one who defined his past three years?

While we are certainly disappointed at Peter's denial of Christ, I am certain that, if we are honest, we can identify with the pressure he felt to do so. Things were not going well for Jesus. Peter's world was swirling, crashing in. Peter, we know, had a family. He had not gone into this week planning to die. He had not been able to prepare himself. With each assertion that he was one of Jesus' followers, with each finger pointed at him, he became more and more anxious, Satan twisted the screws, pushing him toward his downfall. Notice that Mark doesn't put any questions in the mouths of those who accuse him of being a disciple of Christ. They

rather insist that he is. In a fit of madness—and that is what
it is, to deny one's Savior, one's Way, Truth, and Life, to sever
ties with the Creator—he broke. He became angry. He called
down a curse on himself—how appropriate! He swore that he
didn't know this Jesus they were talking so much about.
He hit his low point, or so he thought. At that point, the
words Jesus had spoken sank in. Jesus had told him he would
betray Him, and he had denied he would. Likely he thought
Jesus was the one who had gone mad. And yet here he
was, Jesus words fulfilled. The law seized him. He was overcome with guilt. He began to weep. Right then, right there.
What a sight to see. What had overcome him? He had overcome himself. He had lost hold of the Savior. In a moment,
everything he believed and valued had been overturned, and
he was thus overcome. He wept. All he had left was shame,
and with that, Mark has us race on and leave Peter behind.

Sinners Shout for Our Convenient Redemption

Mark 15:6-15

As much as it pains us, here we must join the throng. Surely their words sting in our ears: "Crucify! Crucify!" And yet, don't we need to join in, in silent prayer, at least, if not with shouts? There is no other salvation than this one, worked through the cross to which Jesus draws near. Humanity is and remains lost without it. Only through God's death can humanity have life, crazy as that sounds. Even if we should try to stop it, even if we reason with His most unreasonable enemies, with which we were numbered by our first birth, He would ignore us. He loves us too much to listen. Like Peter, we would find only a rebuke. Our thoughts are not His thoughts. Our ways are not His ways. We might protest, but "Get behind me, Satan!" is all He would have to say to us in reply. Sinners shout for our convenient redemption. It will keep the peace, the leaders argued. And it will do more than that. It will give the peace, the peace of God, which surpasses our understanding, boggles our finite minds, to those who hunger and thirst for it, who have not and cannot find it in anything else. So get ready. Bring yourself to say it: "Crucify." You may not will it, but God does, not for Himself, but for us. The Lamb goes uncomplaining forth, and while we sinners drive Him forward with our shouting, His love, so strong no words can at this point do it justice, pulls Him silently forward. All this He does to put new words in our mouths, to give us life to shout instead of death.

Mockers Confess the Christ

Mark 15:16-20

Mark's Gospel is full of irony. A number of times Christ's enemies accuse Him of doing the very thing they are doing: blaspheming, disobeying God, serving the devil, and so on. Mark's sense for irony is readily apparent as we now meet His first mockers and abusers on this homestretch to the cross. They mock Him for what He indeed is. They confess Him, although not in faith, and certainly not with any good intention. Sometimes very well-meaning Christians sound the alarm that the church is dying. They wring their hands and furiously plot its rescue, brainstorming to find the next big gimmick or program. Remember that even these heathen, malicious, sadistic torturers and mockers of our Jesus were moved to confess, whether they realized it or not. The gospel, the truth of Christ, is bigger than all of us and can turn even the most twisted persecutors of the faith into preachers, at least for a moment. See your Sinner King, arrayed in purple, crowned with thorns, with sinners kneeling before Him, and remember that, no matter what. God will have His message proclaimed and the Gospel will find mouths and ears until Christ's return.

Jesus here drew the attention of a whole battalion of Gentile sinners. To them, He was just a foolish Jew, a religious fanatic, and yet for them, He was the Savior of Jew and Gentile, the end of the division between the two, the new temple. They dressed Jesus in a purple robe, the color of royalty, an expensive dye that could produce powerful hues. They crowned Him with thorns—Adam's curse, our curse. He became our Sinner King, taking on Himself the consequences of our fall to make us partakers of His Ascension. They saluted Him and confessed correctly, though without faith and with only ill intention, "Hail, King of the Jews!" (15:18 ESV). They hit him and spat on him and knelt down, as every knee will do at the name of Jesus, in artificial homage. Here is humanity's welcome to its King and Savior. Christ has come to redeem us, and all we have to offer is derision. And not much has changed. The Gospel still often evokes the same response today, derision and scorn, laughter and nastiness. Finally, they stripped Him and put Him back in His own clothes, and in Mark's typical fashion, he simply ends this passage, "And they led Him out to crucify Him" (15:20 ESV). In the Jordan, Christ had become the sinner, received a sinner's baptism. Now, after His coronation as the Sinner King, He is led out to a sinner's cross, *our* cross.

The Day We Died

Mark 15:21–41

So where is the sinner in this part of our race? Who do we meet next? Here it gets difficult. Here we meet, not another, but ourselves. Yes, we encounter a few we do well to take note of, but we fail the task before us as we behold Christ's crucifixion if we don't see ourselves in it all. Here we see the end result of our every wayward thought, word, or deed. Here we meet the wages of our sin. Here we see ourselves, in the person of Christ, getting our just deserts. Here we see our cross, and yet we are not on it. There is no such thing as cheap grace. Grace cost God His life, caused His blood to baptize Calvary's head, held the Savior to this tree. Here we see ourselves, and we are tempted to avert our gaze, but we dare not do so.

Hear the Savior's cry: "My God, my God, why have you forsaken me?" (15:34). Why had God forsaken Him? God forsaking God? For *me*, for *you*. He who had no sin suffers our hell, the hell of all sinners, to bring us heaven. He is forsaken so that we can never claim that God has forsaken us. Dark as our nights, God is there. When He seems farthest away, He is often nearest. This torturous tree is a reminder of that, and it marks our lives. We cannot escape it. The crosses we bear for Him are gracious reminders of it. After Good Friday comes Easter, but only after Good Friday. After death, life, but only after death. Here we die with Jesus so we can rise with him, justified through His resurrection.

Did you notice how bare-bones Mark's account is of the crucifixion? Here's what happened, he says. He leaves out a lot. We meet the thief on the cross as a mocker, but he does not, like Luke, include the account of his conversion. The women only are mentioned after His death. There is no mention of John. He does note that the curtain of the temple was torn in two—Christ had removed the barrier between God and men; our sins are forgiven! He also provides one more confession from the lips of a sinner, although we don't know the degree to which he understood his own words. The centurion confesses, "Surely this man was the Son of God!" (15:39). And He *is* the Son of God. God came to earth and we killed Him. And yet He *is* the Son of God. Even dead and carried to His tomb, even buried in it, He *is* the Son of God, for me and for you.

We also meet Simon of Cyrene. Mark doesn't tell us much about him. Mark just tells us what he did. He was forced to help Christ carry his cross. For all we know, he had no clue of who Jesus was before this, and yet he finds himself with Jesus in His darkest hour, intimately, precisely at the climax of Jesus' time with us. Simon helped Jesus carry the cross so Jesus wouldn't die before they nailed Him to it. He helped prolong the Savior's suffering, and yet what he did will forever be remembered as an unwanted and very likely begrudging act of love. He helped Jesus bear up under the wood of our salvation. He kept Jesus moving to the finish line of our redemption. He didn't save us, and he didn't want to be there, but God used him. And whatever took place that day, it bore fruit in Simon's life. We don't know if he became a Christian, but his sons sure seem to have become followers of the one their father followed under the cross. They followed Jesus under their crosses as Simon had followed Jesus under His, but in an even greater fashion, by and through faith, granted them by the Spirit. And so Mark, who doesn't add in details just for fun, writes that Simon was "the father of Alexander and Rufus" (15:21).

We aren't called to help Christ carry His cross. That is finished. Our redemption is done. Our salvation is accomplished. Forgiveness is ours. We are justified. And yet, like Alexander and Rufus, Christ's call to us is the same. In the middle of Mark's Gospel, the Evangelist included some important words of Jesus':

> If anyone would come after me, let him deny himself and take up his cross and follow me. For whoever would save his life will lose it, but whoever loses his life for my sake and the gospel's will save it. For what does it profit a man to gain the whole world and forfeit his soul? For what can a man give in return for his soul? For whoever is ashamed of me and of my words in this adulterous and sinful generation, of him will the Son of Man also be ashamed when he comes in the glory of his Father with the holy angels.

Just as the cross marked our head and heart in Baptism, so it defines our lives, even as it will one day adorn our grave. We are people of the cross, and sometimes God allows us to carry crosses, for His sake, and for our benefit. The flesh still hangs around our neck. The old Adam still lingers. And so through suffering—suffering that often is not a direct consequence of our sin and not in any way our fault—Christ mortifies our flesh, even as He put death to death, through the cross. And throughout it all, we hold fast to what has brought us here: His promises. The Gospel sinks its fingers into us at such time and refuses to let go, even when it sounds distant. Christ is there, as Simon of Cyrene was for Him, to help us bear up, to help us finish our race, not for heaven, but to the heaven that He has won and prepared for us, not as a result of our works, but as a gift. That gift remains ours throughout our trials, and it always remains a gift, even when we give all for Christ, and that is what imbues our suffering with purpose, unlike the unbeliever's, even though we certainly need not court trial and tribulation. And in the midst of it all, we know that none of it can kill us. It can only make us stronger. For we have been crucified with Christ, and we now live by faith in Him, who is greater than our hearts and strong in our weakness, confident that He who was forsaken for us will never forsake us, that He has stretched out His arms in death to lay hold of us and bring us—sometimes kicking and screaming, sometimes bruised and bloodied, yes, at times even near faithless and frantic—to life in abundance everlasting. He *is* the Son of God, and He is with us, and He is for us, with this love, the love that held Him to the tree.

And Peter

Mark 16:1–8

The apostles are nowhere to be found, as at the cross, with the exception of John. They are huddled in fear. They are reeling. Their thoughts run into each other when they aren't too numb to think. But here are the women, again. Here are the women, devoted to Jesus, even as they think He is dead, dead as a doornail, dead dead. They've come to anoint Him. They don't want His body to stink. Perhaps this is to be their last act of devotion for the Master. Oh, how they missed Him! Perhaps, like the Emmaus disciples, they spoke in a past tense that would have pulled at the Savior's heart. They *had* thought He *was* the One who was going to deliver Israel. Boy, were they in for a surprise!

When they got to the tomb, they wondered how they would get to Jesus, who would roll away the stone. Someone had already thought of that, though. The stone was removed for them, even though, as Mark notes, it was very large. Even more, there was someone waiting, and it *wasn't* a deceased Rabbi. It was a young man. Some theologians speculate it was the same young man who had fled naked. (They argue that wasn't Mark and draw some interesting connections, with which we will not busy ourselves here, first, because I don't buy it, at least at this point, and second, because, like Mark, I don't want to weary you with words and unnecessary detail at this point.) Regardless, Mark writes, "And entering the tomb, they saw a young man sitting on the right side, dressed in a white robe, and they were alarmed" (16:5). And why wouldn't they be alarmed? This was a curveball. This wasn't on their radar, as much as maybe it should have been, since the Lord hadn't hidden what would happen from His disciples.

Mark now gives us two verses full of beautiful words. In typical fashion, he packs power into a very brief passage. Here we have, with the crucifixion, the central event of human history, and Mark tells it in what could be one paragraph, and not a very long one, and the young man drives home what it means and what should follow in just a few sentences. This account is brimming with beautiful words, but I am convinced two are the most beautiful.

"Don't be afraid." Those are beautiful words. They sum up the gospel. Don't be afraid, for He said all along this would happen. Death has lost its sting. Christ destroyed it by enduring it. Hell now has no hold on you. Christ descended to slam shut its gates. How could you be afraid? Our Jesus lives! Don't be afraid! These are beautiful words.

"He is risen" (16:6). Those are beautiful words too. He is risen, and the devil is cast down. He is risen, and sin is buried. He is risen, and death has died. He is risen, and life springs forth from the grave. He is risen! These are beautiful words.

"Just as He said" (16:6). Certainly, these are beautiful words. Jesus kept His promises. His Word is bond. Faith does not deal with potentialities. What God says is as good as done. What beautiful words!

But these still aren't the words I have in mind. The beautiful words I have in mind might not even have stood out to you, but they should have. Those beautiful words are "and Peter" (16:7). Those are the words I can't get out of my head. "Go, tell His disciples and Peter" (16:7). Do me a favor, read them once again, but this time insert your name. And *Wade*. And *you*.

Think of Peter. He had betrayed His Lord just a little while after promising to follow Him even unto death. He'd failed the Savior. His big moment of testing came and he flunked. And now it was too late. His Master was dead and buried. There was no opportunity to make things better, to apologize. But thanks be to God! Unbeknownst to Peter, His Master was dead and buried no more. He had risen, just as He said, and before Peter could apologize, Christ had already made sure that the good news of His resurrection was announced, not just to all of the disciples, but especially to him. "And Peter."

"Et tu, Brute?" "And you, Brutus?" Those were the words Shakespeare had Caesar speak when he realized that even his best friend was conspiring to take his life. The friendship ended in betrayal. But Christ now has the angel speak His "And you" in a different tone and to a different end. These are words of friendship and love. The friendship did not end with Peter's betrayal. It is born anew through Christ's forgiving love, doubtless more powerful than ever.

The early church and most scholars today worth the price of their books are confident that Mark wrote his Gospel based on the preaching of Peter. So far as I can tell, the "and Peter" appears only in St. Mark's Gospel. I find this mesmerizing. Peter himself likely preached this "and Peter," confessing the mercy of Christ shortly after confessing the sin of his betrayal. How beautiful! It makes sense that such a message would stick with Mark because, as we discussed, he was perhaps (likely) the same youth, recorded only in Mark's Gospel, who fled naked from Gethsemane when Christ was betrayed, so frightened that he left his robe behind when they seized him. In Peter's account of the "and Peter" spoken to the women, Mark, together with every sinner hungry and thankful for forgiveness, would have heard an "and Mark" as well. I pray you hear an "and you."

The apostles hadn't exactly been stalwart in their faith the past few days. In fact, they remained impressively unimpressive up to the point Jesus appeared to them. The women muster up the courage and head out to anoint their dead Rabbi as the big bad fishermen cower and hide. The women brave the prospect of a huge rock and ornery Roman soldiers. It's a good thing Jesus wasn't still in His grave, or He likely would have been rolling over in it. But still, Christ is sure to have this angel tell the women to "go and tell His disciples and Peter" (16:7). Christ does not hold a grudge. In fact, He died to let grudges go. And He sought out those apostles again and sent *them* out in His name as His spokesmen, as His brothers.

The resurrection is about new life, especially eternal life, but the resurrection is about new life here and now as well. Buried with Christ in Baptism, we now rise to new life in Him who died to give it to us. Where before, only we who were involved in decisions and only our own self-interest was there to motivate us, so now there is a new Man and an eternal gratitude.

"And Peter." Death has been swallowed up. Our long-awaited salvation has arrived. The Savior wipes away our tears. On the seventh day God rested. On this first day of a new week, the eighth day, God begins creation anew, raising up again what had fallen into sin, beginning our renewal in His image. Death must now give way to life, sin to grace, fear to comfort, sadness to joy, doubt to conviction, despair to hope, punishment to reward, apologies to forgiveness, and confusion to peace.

"And Peter." "And you." This is your new day. By Christ's resurrection, it's the first day of eternal life. Bury your sin in His empty tomb, because there is plenty of room. He isn't using it anymore. Have you come to the tomb early? Rejoice! Have you come late? Rejoice! Have you come to remember the dead? Rejoice! Have you come seeking the living? Rejoice! Have you come to escape your sin? Rejoice! Have you come to find your forgiveness? Rejoice! Have you come in faith? Rejoice! Have you come looking for something to believe? Rejoice! No matter how you have come, rejoice, for your Jesus lives! He lives, and we receive not dead Body and Blood, but living! He lives, and He lives for you! And you! Beautiful words, aren't they—that "and Peter"?!

Jesus Sends Sinners to Make Saints

Mark 16:14–20

Here we could engage in a rather lengthy debate about whether this section is the actual ending of Mark's original Gospel. We *could* do that. We will not do that. What do I think? It depends on the day. Is anything lost either way? Not anything that isn't made abundantly clear elsewhere in Scripture. Ultimately, the point remains the same no matter what. Jesus told the first witnesses of the resurrection to go and tell. Jesus here tells the disciples the same. Jesus sends sinners to make saints. No, sinners do not make the saints, but Jesus makes them *through their preaching*. Christ has given the Church the Gospel, and the Gospel, the Gospel alone, is its lifeblood and the means through which sinners become saints, through which the dead are raised, through which the lost are found.

At the tomb, we now encounter Mary Magdalen. Out of her, Jesus had cast seven demons. God only knows the words that came out of her mouth before He had done so, when she was under the power of the evil one. But, oh, the words that come out of her mouth now! She proclaims the resurrection. She brings the good news to those who had been with Him, to His disciples. She brings glad tidings into the midst of mourning and weeping, hope into an abyss of despair. And yet the disciples were slow to believe. It was too much. This week had been a rollercoaster. Could they take another twist?

Jesus next appeared to two disciples as they walked along a path into the countryside, likely those to whom Luke introduces us on the road to Emmaus. They too went from what might have been to what is, from sorrow to joy, and hurried to tell their brothers. But what do we read? Still the others were slow to believe. People don't just rise from the dead. There seemed to be no way to pull them out of their grief.

Finally, Christ Himself appeared to the eleven. He rebuked them. They had fallen into unbelief. Their hearts had become coarse. And yet He didn't send them away. He commissioned them. He sent *them* to proclaim the good news they were so slow to believe to all the world. He sent sinners to sinners to make saints. He set their tongues loose, and set them loose to declare what Christ had declared to them, a righteousness not from within but from outside, not of our own but the gift of God, from God and of God. He left no doubt how we are saved. He stated without equivocation: "Whoever believes and is baptized will be saved, but whoever does not believe will be condemned" (16:16). And nothing has changed, and so we do well to be a people about the Gospel, a church faithful to its purpose, preaching and baptizing, setting forth the love of our crucified God in doctrine and life, at the font, the altar, and the pulpit, in our homes. This is where Christ is with us, and not only with us but *with us for us*. This is where Christ still meets sinners, outcasts, and untouchables, and takes hold of them, sticks his fingers in their ears, opens their eyes, spits on their tongues, and draws them into His company—even His family—and sets them free to live lives of love and hope and faithfulness, going forth in the victory of a race finished down a path still strewn with sinners loved by Christ, of which we are, and for whom He has given himself.

40365376R00066

Made in the USA
Middletown, DE
26 March 2019